Access 2007

Right from the Start

R. Chasemore

www.harcourt.co.uk
✓ Free online support
✓ Useful weblinks
✓ 24 hour online ordering

01865 888070

PAYNE-GALLWAY

Payne-Gallway is an imprint of Harcourt Education Limited, a company incorporated in England and Wales, having its registered office: Halley Court, Jordan Hill, Oxford OX2 8EJ. Registered company number: 3099304

www.harcourt.co.uk

First published 2007

12 11 10 09 08 07
10 9 8 7 6 5 4 3 2 1

British Library Cataloguing in Publication Data is available from the British Library on request.

ISBN 978 1 905292 36 3

Edited by John Giles
Typeset by Sparks, Oxford – www.sparks.co.uk
Cover design by Peter Stratton
Cover photo/illustration ©iStockPhotos/WaD
Printed in China by South China Printing Co. Ltd.

Acknowledgements

The author and publisher would like to thank the following individuals and organisations for permission to reproduce screenshots:

Microsoft product screenshots reprinted with permission from Microsoft

Every effort has been made to contact copyright holders of material reproduced in this book. Any omissions will be rectified in subsequent printings if notice is given to the publishers.

Websites

The websites used in this book were correct and up-to-date at the time of publication. It is essential for tutors to preview each website before using it in class so as to ensure that the URL is still accurate, relevant and appropriate. We suggest that tutors bookmark useful websites and consider enabling students to access them through the school/college intranet.

Ordering Information
Payne-Gallway, FREEPOST (OF1771),
PO Box 381, Oxford OX2 8BR
Tel: 01865 888070
Fax: 01865 314029
Email: orders@payne-gallway.co.uk

Contents

Chapter 1 – Introduction to Databases 4

Chapter 2 – Creating a New Database 9

Chapter 3 – Datasheet View 21

Chapter 4 – Data Validation 30

Chapter 5 – Sorting, Formatting and Printing Tables 35

Chapter 6 – Making Queries 40

Chapter 7 – Presenting Data 47

Chapter 8 – Relational Database Design 56

Chapter 9 – Creating Tables 62

Chapter 10 – Setting up Relationships 70

Chapter 11 – Forms and Command Buttons 75

Chapter 12 – Forms and Subforms 87

Chapter 13 – Advanced Queries 99

Chapter 14 – Reports 104

Chapter 15 – Creating a Menu 114

Index 120

Chapter 1 – Introduction to Databases

Note:
To begin with we will look at databases containing just one table. Later we will create one with many tables.

What is Microsoft Access?

Microsoft Access is one of the most widely used database packages. Databases are used to store large amounts of information, and allow you to sort and filter the information or **data** to provide useful reports.

A database is based on tables of data, and each table contains many fields.

This is an example of how an art collection might look in a table of data:

Name of Painting	Artist	Gallery
Acuminatus	Mark Johnston	CCA Galleries
The North Unfolds	Neil Canning	Martin Tinney Gallery
Heat of the Day	Claire Blois	Kilmorack Gallery
Two Birches	James Hawkins	Rhue Studio

Table 1.1

? How many columns are there in the table?

? How many rows are there in the table?

Answers:

✓ There are 3 columns. The column headings are the **field names**, so there are 3 fields in the table.

✓ There are 4 rows. The rows are the records, so there are 4 **records** in this table.

Each time the art collector purchases a new painting, he can catalogue it by adding a new record to the table.

The art collector can use the database to find out information such as:

- whether he owns a particular painting
- which paintings he has by Neil Canning
- which gallery a particular painting came from
- how many paintings he has from a particular gallery
- the artist of a particular painting.

Databases are not often used for such small amounts of data, because the answers to the above questions can be easily answered just by looking at the table. However, if you had hundreds of paintings there would be hundreds of rows, and the table would be so big it would take hours to answer the questions. This is where a database becomes very useful.

Before creating a database on the computer it is important to **plan** your database.

Planning a database

When planning a database you need to think about the answers to these questions:

- What is the purpose of the database?
- What information will you want to look up in the database?
- What data will you store in the database?

House builder database

First you are going to design a database for a house builder, Bentwells, that is starting a new development called Neventown Gardens. Bentwells needs the database to keep track of all its customers.

Purpose of the database

The sales staff need to be able to find out quickly and easily:

- which customers are interested in a particular plot
- which customers are interested in a particular style or price of house
- who has already reserved a particular plot
- how many people have registered an interest in each plot
- the contact number and address of a particular customer.

After talking to the sales staff in Bentwells, you have found out the following:

- There will be a total of 30 plots on the new Neventown Gardens development.
- The development will consist only of detached houses, with 3–5 bedrooms.
- The price of a property depends on the style of house. All plots with the same style of house are the same price.
- A customer must pay £250 to reserve a plot (each plot can only be reserved by one customer).
- There are several phases in purchasing a house: registering interest in a particular plot, reserving a plot, exchange of contracts and completion.

Tip:
Remember that the fields in the table are the column headings.

Your database should contain details on each customer and the properties they are interested in. The next step is to decide which **fields** to have in your table. Based on the information given above, the table must contain the following information about each customer:

- name
- contact number
- plot interested in
- plot style
- plot price
- stage of purchase (interested, reserved, exchanged, completed)
- exchange date
- deposit paid Y/N
- total amount paid.

These pieces of information will make up the basis of the fields in your table.

Data types

Before you can set up these fields in your database, you need to think about what format the data will be in. Access has many different **data types**, which are explained in the table below:

Text	Letters, symbols and numbers, i.e. Alphanumeric data.
Number	Numbers only (no letters). Includes numbers with decimal points.
Date/Time	Dates and times.
Currency	For all monetary data. Access will insert a currency symbol before the amount (such as £ or $, etc.)
Yes/No	Used wherever the field can be one of only 2 values, Y/N, True/False, Male/Female, etc.
AutoNumber	This is a unique value generated by Access for each record.

Table 1.2

Deciding on data types

You will have to choose a data type for each field from the table given above. For example, should you hold a telephone number as a **Text** field or a **Number** field? At first you may think that a **Number** field would be best but in practice this is a bad idea for two reasons:

- Access will not record leading zeroes in a number field. So if the telephone number is 0149450 it will be recorded as 149450 which is incorrect.

- Access will not allow you to put a space, bracket or hyphen in a number field. So you will not be able to record a telephone number as, for example, 01473 874512.

Selecting fields

We already have a list that will form the basis of the fields in the database (name, contact number, etc.). You may now wish to split some of the pieces of information, for example, name will include a *first name* and a *surname*. Should you split this into two fields? There are two main reasons why you may wish to do this:

- If you want to sort the customers alphabetically by surname, this is much easier to do if **Surname** is a separate field.
- You may wish to search for a particular customer record. It will be much easier to search on the surname.

Designing the database structure

The structure of the database can be thought of as what the table will look like without any information in (i.e. the design of the table). To describe the structure you need to know:

- how many fields the table will have (the columns in the table)
- what will be the field names (the column headings)
- what data type will be held in each field.

The number of rows will change as the user enters more data, and is not part of the database structure.

It is important to know the difference between the **database structure** (think of the empty table) and the **data** held in the database (the information that you put into the table).

For each of the following changes to the **Painting** database in Table 1.1, would you need to change the database structure or edit the data?

- You decide to add a new field name, **Price**, to the database.
- The painting **Two Birches** was actually purchased from **Kilmorack Gallery**.

Answers:

- ✓ If you add a new field name, you are changing the database structure.
- ✓ If you are changing the Two Birches record, you are only editing the data.

Naming conventions

We will use a common name notation when naming tables and field names. This means putting **tbl** in front of the table names, and not using any spaces in any of the names. Use capital letters in the middle of a field name to make the words easier to read. Look at the table below to see an example.

tblCustomer

Field Name	Data Type
CustomerID	AutoNumber
Title	Text
Surname	Text
ContactNo	Text
PlotNo	Number
PlotStyle	Text
PlotPrice	Currency
Stage	Text
ExchangeDate	Date/Time
DepositPaid	Y/N

Table 1.3

This will be the database structure of the **Customer** table.

Note: To minimise the amount of data that you will need to enter for this sample database, **FirstName** is omitted, even though it would normally be included.

Note:
You can use letters, numbers, spaces and special characters like? or &. Don't use an exclamation mark (!) or a full stop in a field name.

Chapter 2 – Creating a New Database

Over the next several chapters you'll be creating and developing the **Bentwells Database**.

Using Access 2007

Access 2007 offers the user the opportunity to use pre-formed templates (see Figure 2.2) which can be used directly from the application. This method of working has the advantage of the novice user quickly being able to use the application to produce a database for their needs without having to first develop the necessary design skills and acquire an understanding of how a database works. Hiding the design process has the disadvantage of the user relying on Access to do all of the database design so that a full understanding of how to design a database for a specific purpose is not developed. This book shows you how to design a database without relying on pre-formed templates. Naturally this will at first be a slower process, but will enable you to use the application in a much more flexible way.

Loading Access

You can load Access in one of two ways:

- Either double-click the **Access** icon on the main screen in Windows

- or click the **Start** button at the bottom left of the screen, then click **Programs**, then click **Microsoft Office Access 2007**:

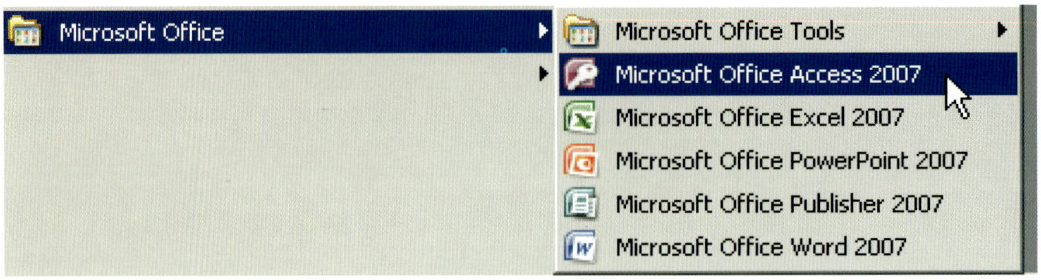

Figure 2.1

Your screen will look like the one below showing the '**Getting Started with Microsoft Office Access**' window:

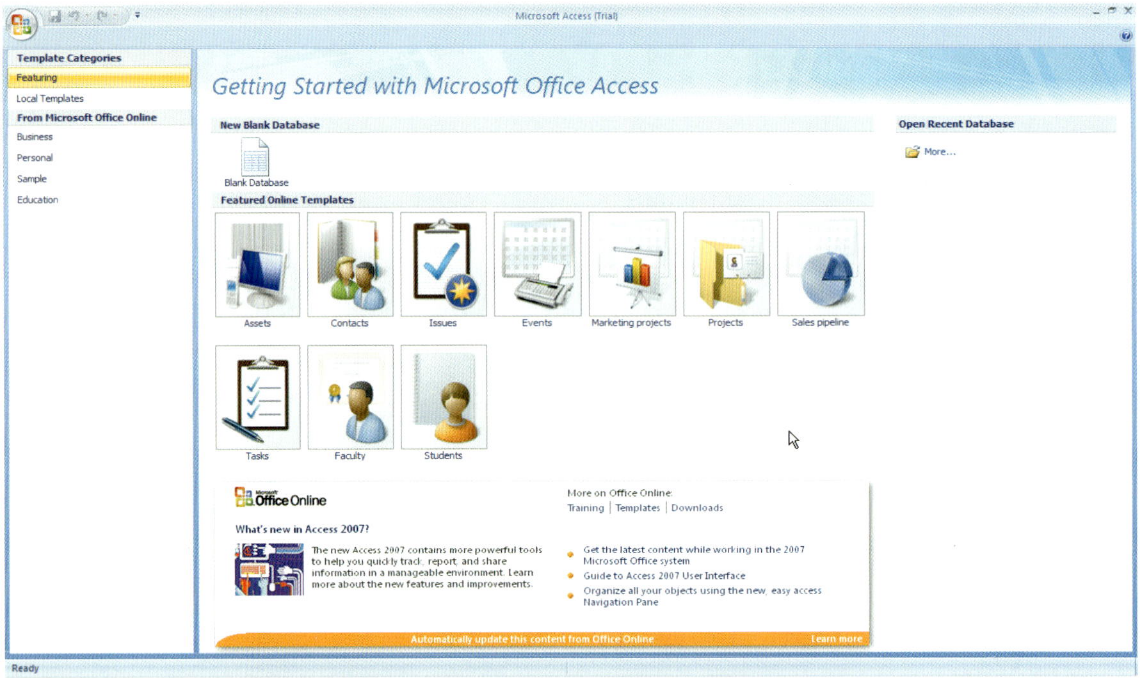

Figure 2.2

You now have the option of either opening an existing database or creating a new one. We will create a new database from scratch.

▶ Click **New Blank Database** in the central pane.

The right-hand pane changes which enables you to either create a new file in the default location used by Access or to select a new location and folder for the new file. We are going to create a new folder for the database, so look at the next figure of the lower right-hand pane:

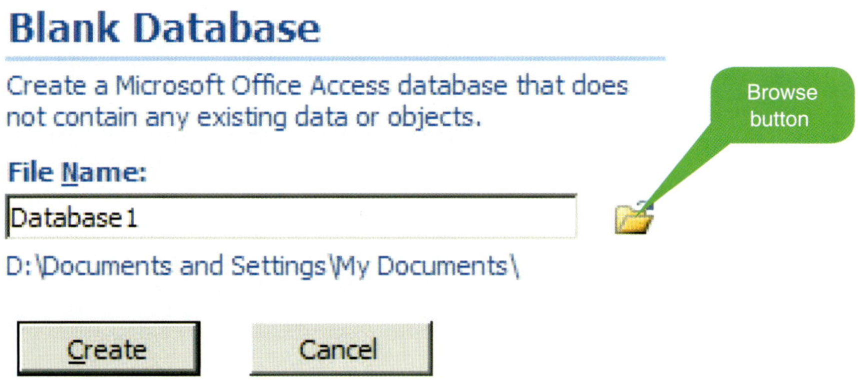

Figure 2.3

- Click the browse button shown in Figure 2.3. The **File New Database** dialogue box opens:

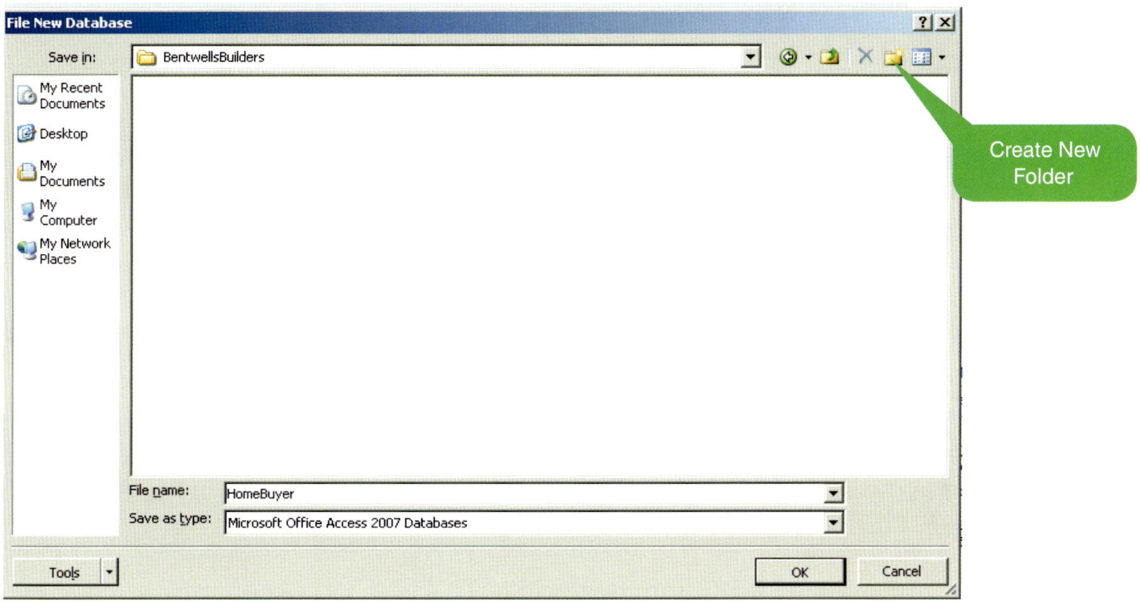

Figure 2.4

- Click the **Create New Folder** button and in the **New Folder** dialogue box name the new folder **BentwellsBuilders** and click **OK**.
- In the **File name** box, type the name **HomeBuyer** (no spaces), and click the **OK** button. Access will automatically add the file extension **.accdb** which you can see in the **File Name** box when Access returns to the original '**Getting Started with Microsoft Office Access**' window:

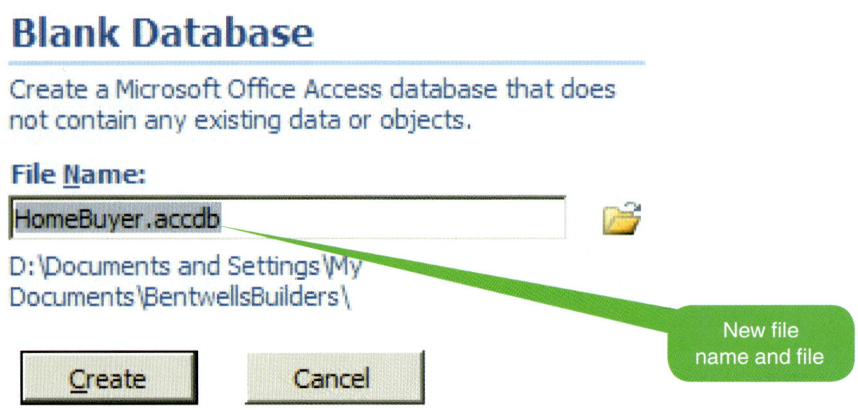

Figure 2.5

Tip:
It is a good idea to keep each Access database in its own folder.

Click **Create**.

The database structure

The first thing you have to do is set up the database structure. As you learned in the first chapter, all data in an Access database is stored in tables. Each table has a row for each record and a column for each field. The first thing you have to do is tell Access exactly what fields you want in each record, and what data type each field is. After this has been done and the structure is saved, you can start adding data to the database.

The Database window

Access databases are made up of **objects**. A **table** is an object, and is the only object we have talked about so far. Other objects, which you will come across in this book, include **Queries, Forms** and **Reports**.

Every Access database has a **Database window**. This is a sort of central menu for your database, from which you can open the objects in your database. The **Database window** has a '**Ribbon**' running across the top from which it is possible to find and develop the objects which you incorporate into your database.

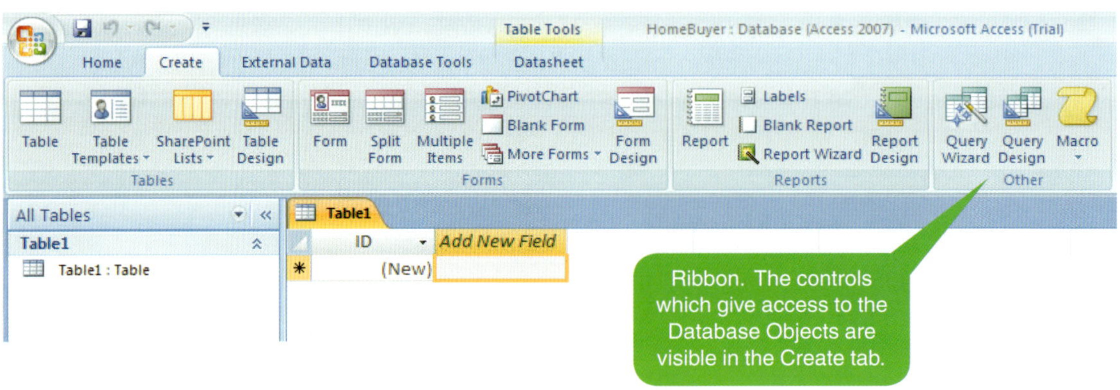

Figure 2.6

Creating a new table

The database opens to show the **Table** database object. Most database objects exist in two views: a **Design View** in which you can change the object to correspond to your requirements and a **Run Time View** which displays the data in its finished arrangement to the user. In this case, Access has opened the **Table** object because this is where the data will be stored and consequently the most fundamental and important of the database objects. The view chosen is **Datasheet View** which is the '**Run Time View**' for the table. We need to design the table first, so we shall have to change the view of the table to **Design View**.

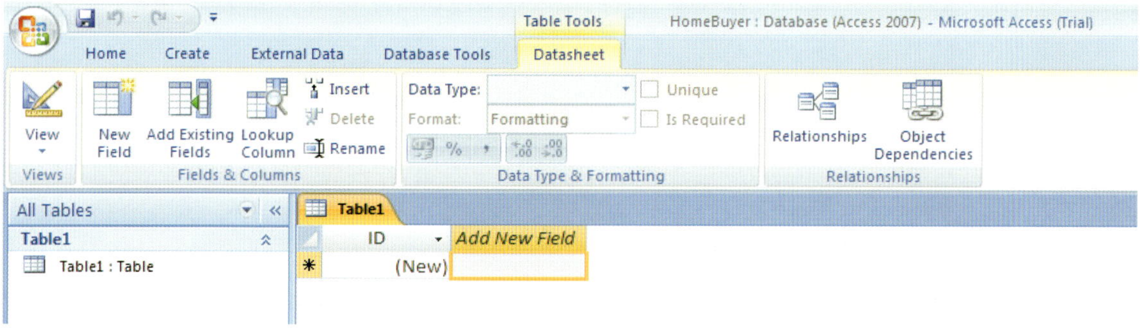

Figure 2.7

- Swap to the **Datasheet** or **Home** tab and then click the **View** button.

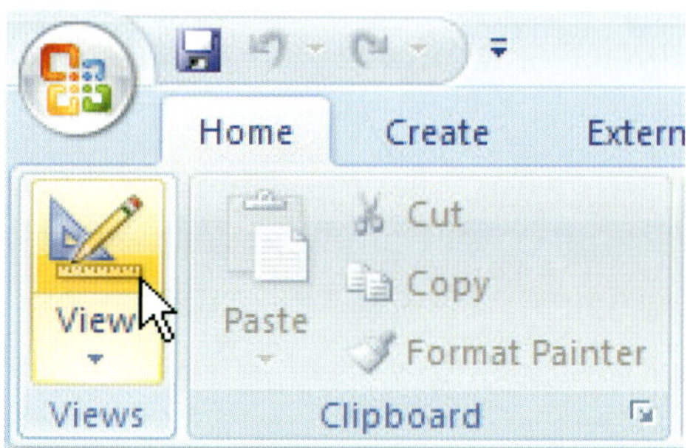

Figure 2.8

- You will be asked to name the table. Type the name **tblCustomer** and click **OK**.

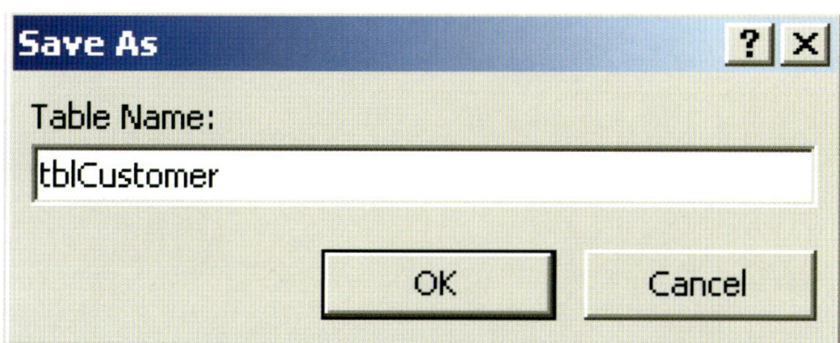

Figure 2.9

The view changes to table design view:

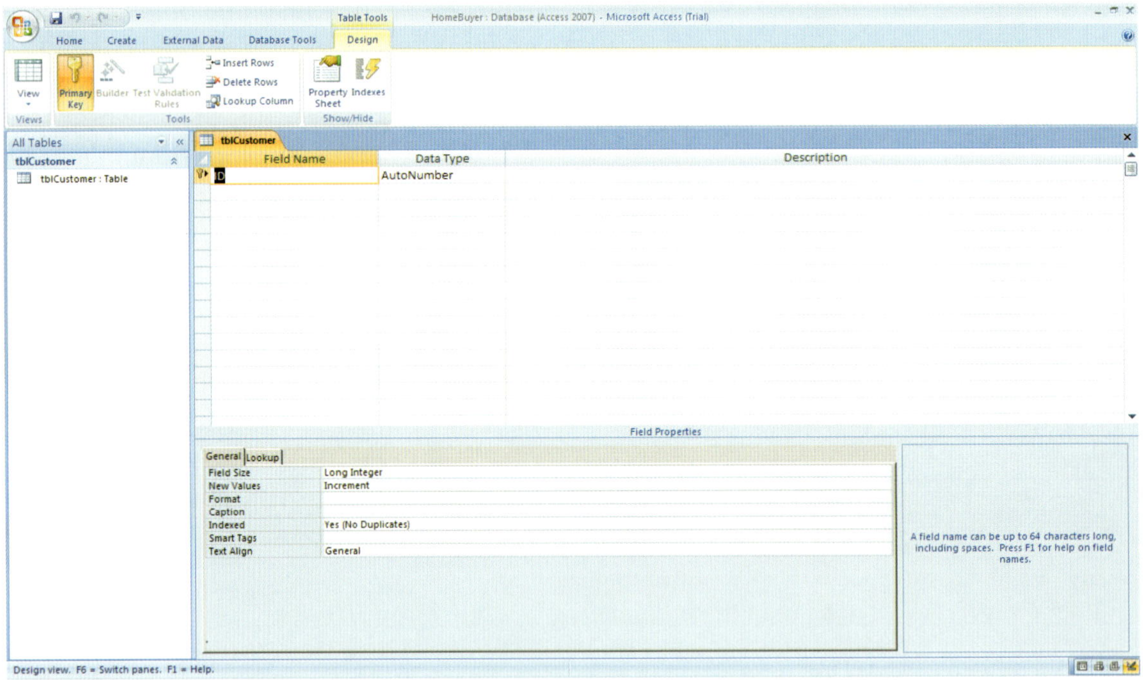

Figure 2.10

Look back at the structure of the **tblCustomer** table in Table 1.3. All these fields need to be entered in the new table.

- In place of the entry 'ID' enter the first field name, **CustomerID**, and tab to the **Data Type** column.
- The data type **AutoNumber** will probably be already offered, but click the down-arrow to see what other data types are available. If **AutoNumber** is not offered, select it now, see Figure 2.11.
- Tab to the **Description** column and type **This is the Key field**.

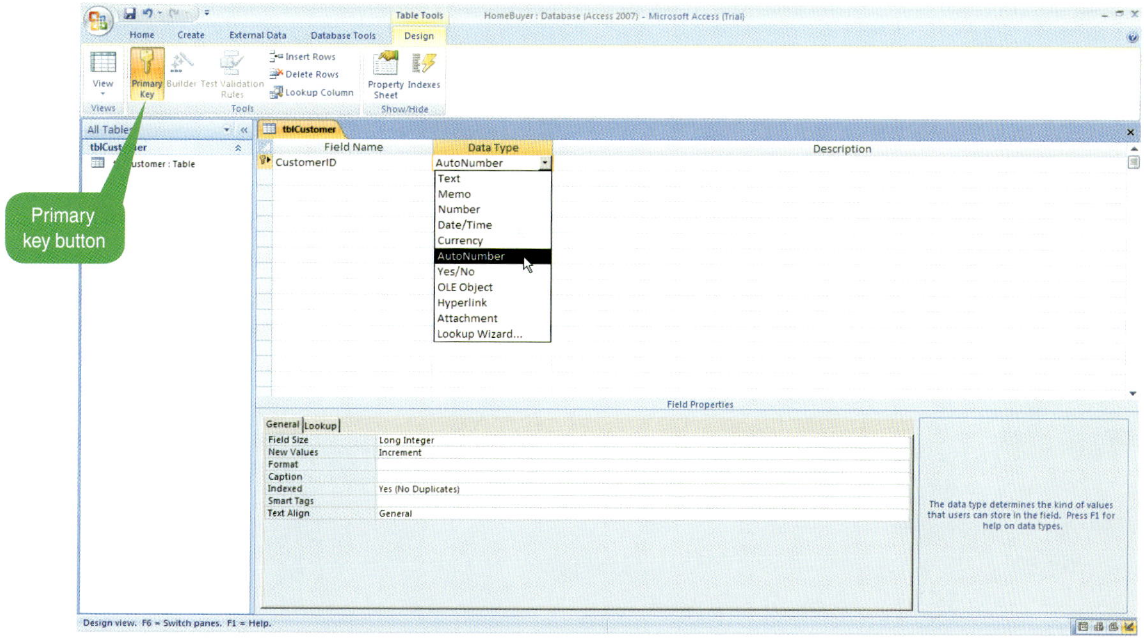

Figure 2.11

Defining the primary key

Every table in an Access database must have a primary key (also known as the key field). The field which you specify for the primary key must have a different value for each record, so that it uniquely identifies a particular record. For the **Customer** database we will set **CustomerID** to be the primary key. We cannot use **Surname** because there may be more than one customer with the same surname.

▶ Access will probably already have offered the first record as the primary key, but if it has not, then with the cursor still in the row for the **CustomerID**, click the **Primary Key** button on the **Table Tools Design** tab of the **Ribbon**. The key symbol appears in the left-hand margin next to the **CustomerID**. This is shown in Figure 2.11.

Entering other fields

Now we can enter all the other fields.

- ▶ In the next row, enter the field name **Title** and leave the data type in the next column as **Text**.
- ▶ Enter the fields for **Surname, ContactNo, PlotNo** and **PlotStyle**. All these fields have a data type **Text** except **PlotNo** which has a data type **Number**.
- ▶ Enter the field name **PlotPrice** and give it a data type of **Currency**.
- ▶ Enter the field name **Stage** and give it a data type of **Text**.
- ▶ Enter the field name **ExchangeDate** give it a data type of **Date/Time**.
- ▶ Enter the field name **DepositPaid** and give it the data type **Yes/No**.

Your table should now look like Figure 2.12:

Tip:
Don't worry if you make a few mistakes – after all the fields are entered, you will learn how to move fields around, delete them or insert new fields. You can correct any mistakes at that point and it will be good practice.

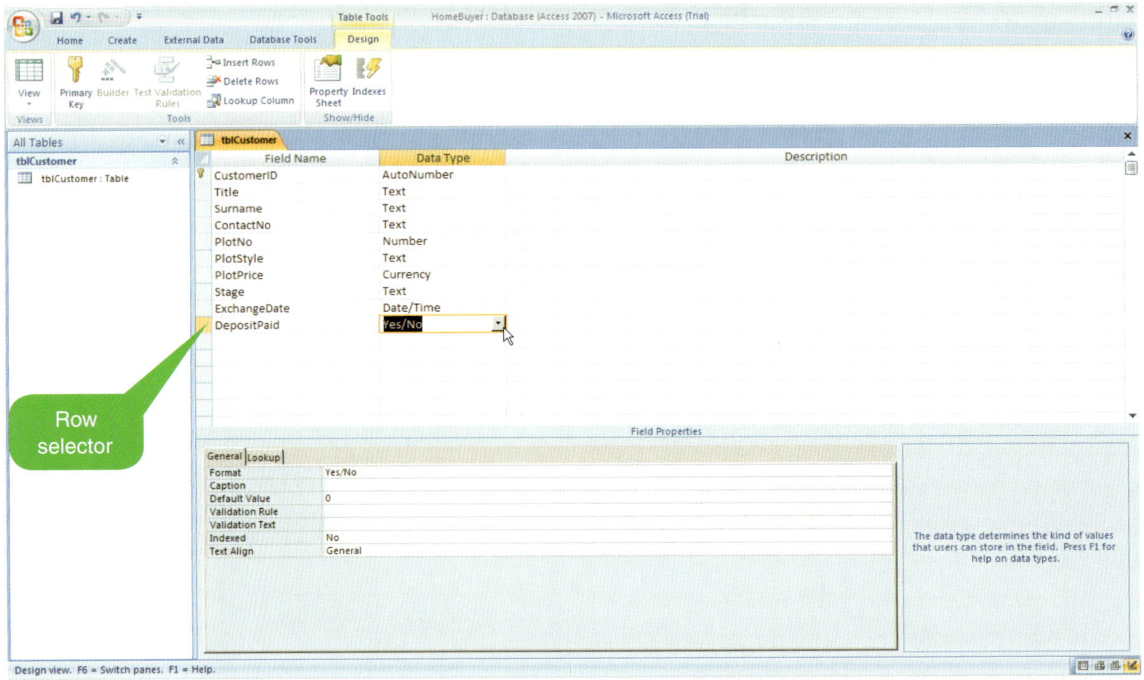

Figure 2.12

Saving the table structure

Click the **Close** icon in the top right-hand corner to close the window. You will be returned to the Database window.

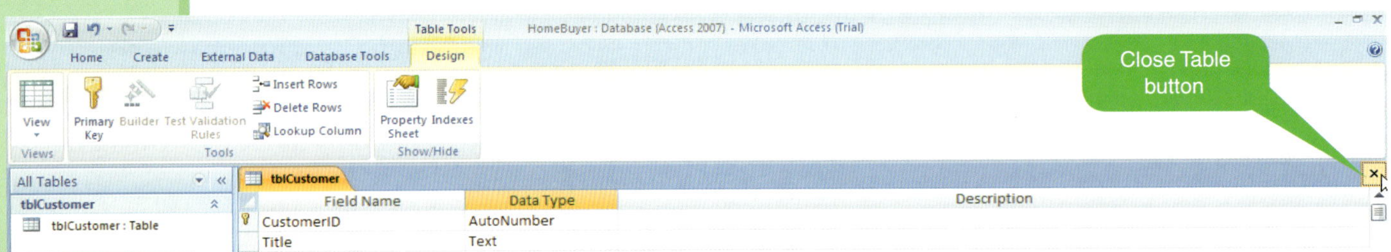

Figure 2.13

You will be asked to confirm that you want to save the changes you have made to the table; of course you do! Click **Yes**.

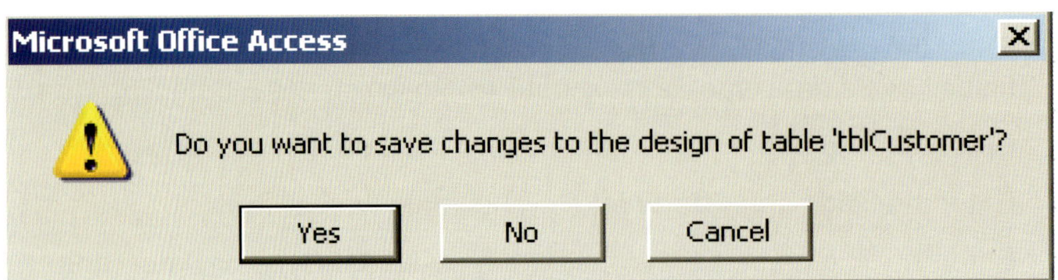

Figure 2.14

Tip:
If you have named the table wrongly, or made a spelling mistake then you can remedy this by using the Navigation pane to the left-hand side of the screen. Right click the name of the table and select Rename from the shortcut menu, then type in the correct name.

Don't worry if you've made some mistakes in the table structure – they can be corrected in a minute.

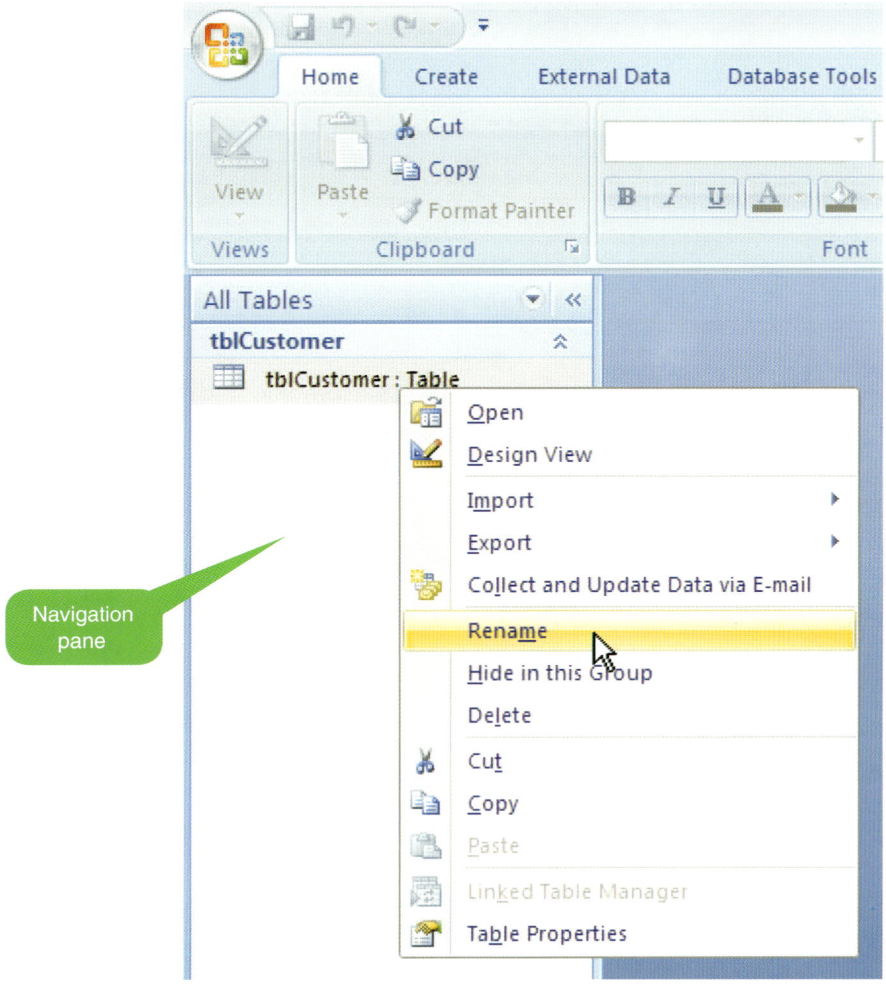

Figure 2.15

Re-opening a table for editing

We are going to practise how to make changes to a table, so we need to open the table again. You can re-open your table from the Navigation pane in two ways:

- **Either** double click the icon next to the table name in the **Navigation** pane, **or**:
- Right click the table icon and select **Open** for **Datasheet** view or select **Design View**.

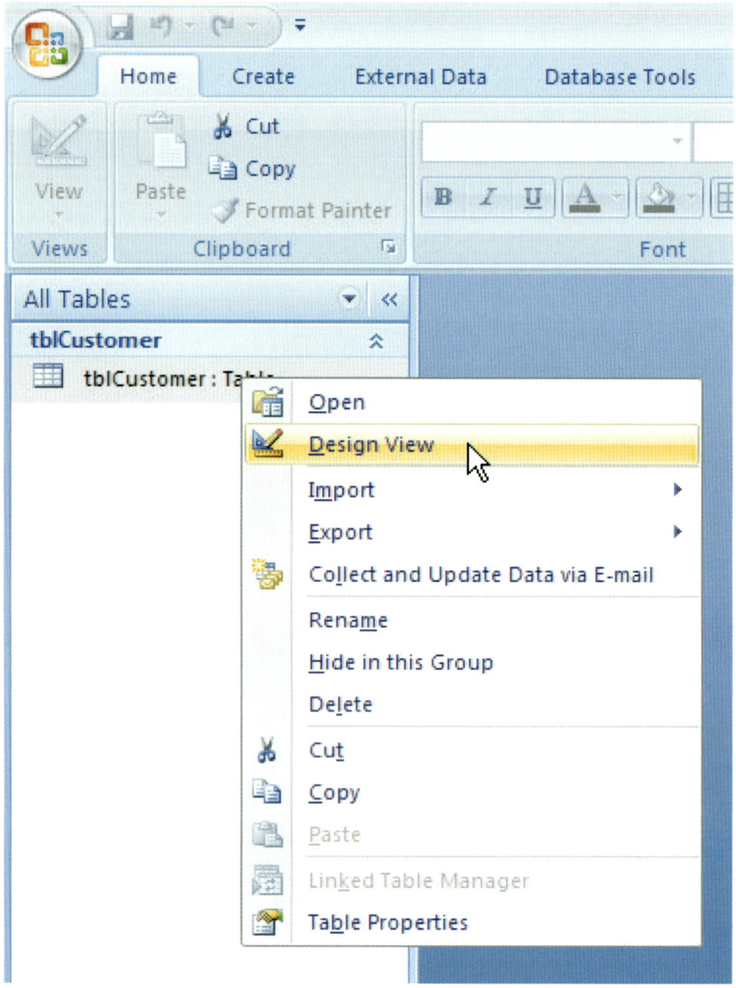

Figure 2.16

Inserting a field

To insert a new row for a second contact number (maybe for a work phone number) just above **PlotNo**:

- Click the row selector (left-hand margin) for **PlotNo**.
- Click the **Insert** key on the keyboard or click the **Insert Rows** button on the **Table Tools Design** tab of the **Ribbon**.

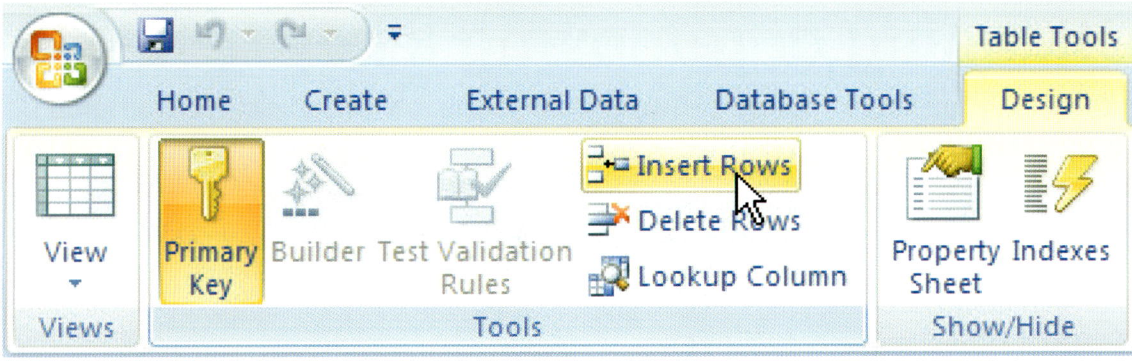

Figure 2.17

- Enter the new field name **ContactWorkNumber**, data type **Text**.

Deleting a field

Now, to delete the field you have just inserted:

- Select the field by clicking in its row selector.
- Click the **Delete** key on the keyboard or click the **Delete Rows** button on the **Table Tools Design** tab of the **Ribbon**.

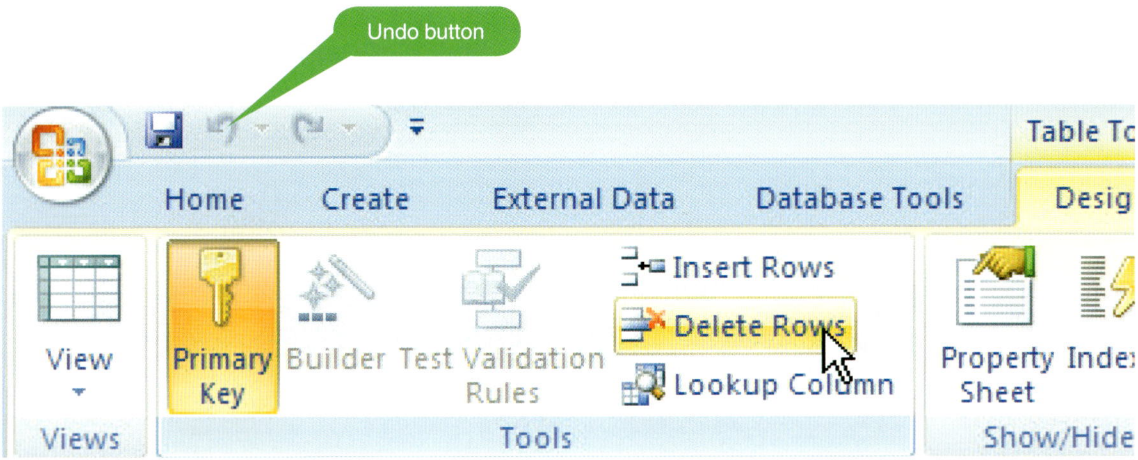

Figure 2.18

If you make a mistake, you can use the **Undo** button on the **Quick Access Toolbar**.

Moving a field

- Click the row selector to the left of the field's name to select the field.
- Click again and drag to where you want the field to be. You will see a line appear between fields as you drag over them to indicate where the field will be placed.

Tip:
The row selector is the square to the left of the field name.

Changing or removing a key field

- To change the key field to **Surname**, click the row selector for the **Surname** field and then click the **Primary Key** button on the **Table Tools Design** tab of the **Ribbon**.
- To remove the primary key altogether, select the row that is currently the key field and click the **Primary Key** button on the **Table Tools Design** tab of the **Ribbon**.

When you have finished experimenting, restore **CustomerID** as the key field of this table. Make any other necessary corrections to leave the fields as specified in Figure 2.12, and save the table structure.

- Save your database by selecting the **File save** button on the **Quick Access Toolbar**.

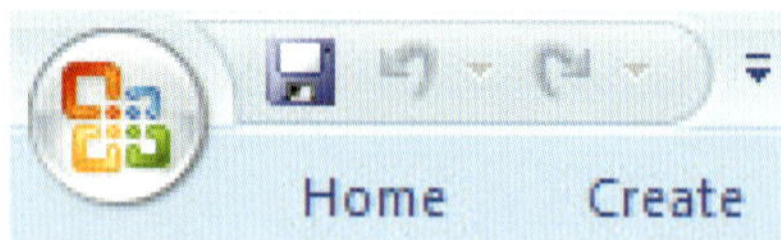

- Close Access using the cross at the right-hand top corner of the database window.

Chapter 3 – Datasheet View

Opening an existing database

- Load Access. The following window will appear.

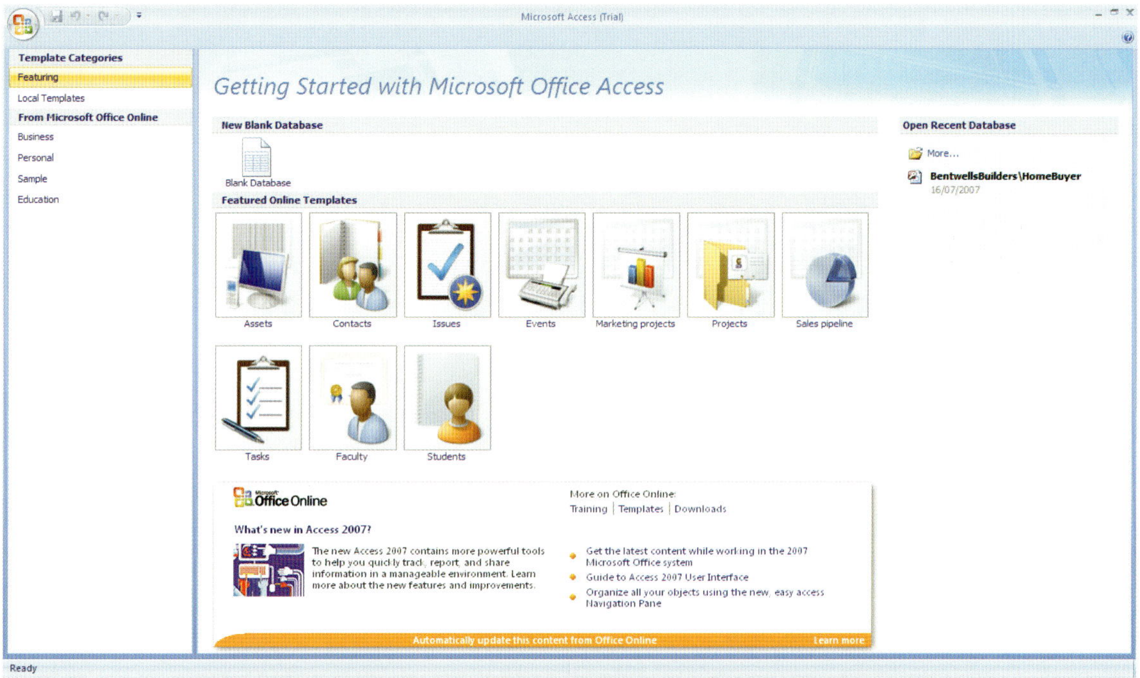

Figure 3.1

- Select **BentwellsBuilders\HomeBuyer** from the right-hand pane. The first name (**BentwellsBuilders**) is the name of the folder which contains the database **HomeBuyer**.

The Database window will appear.

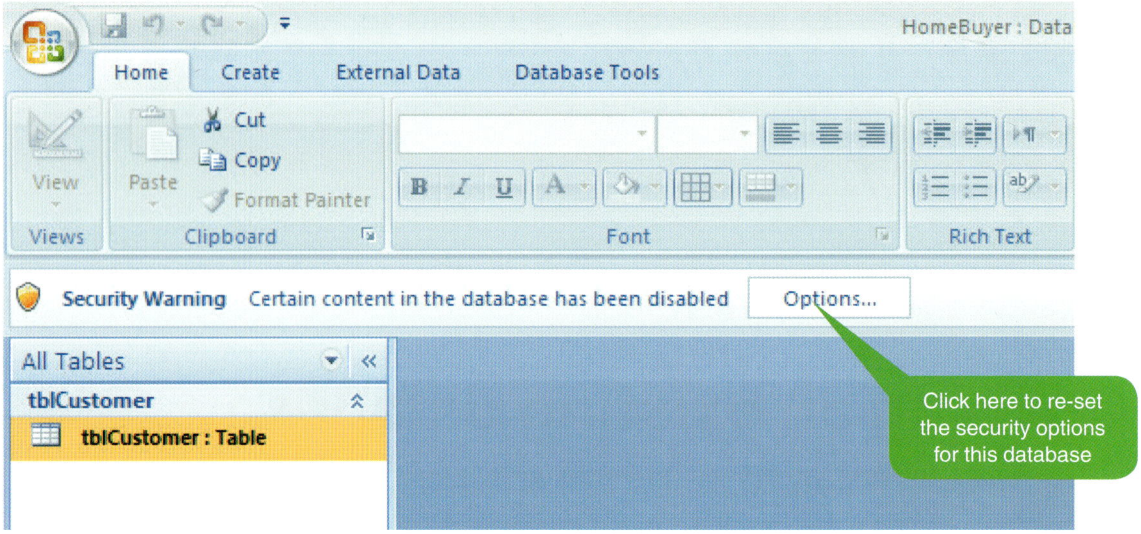

FIgure 3.2

The database will not function correctly until the security options have been re-set.

- Click the **Option** button just to the right of the security warning.
- The **Security Alert** dialogue box appears. Click the radio button '**Enable this content**' and then **OK**.

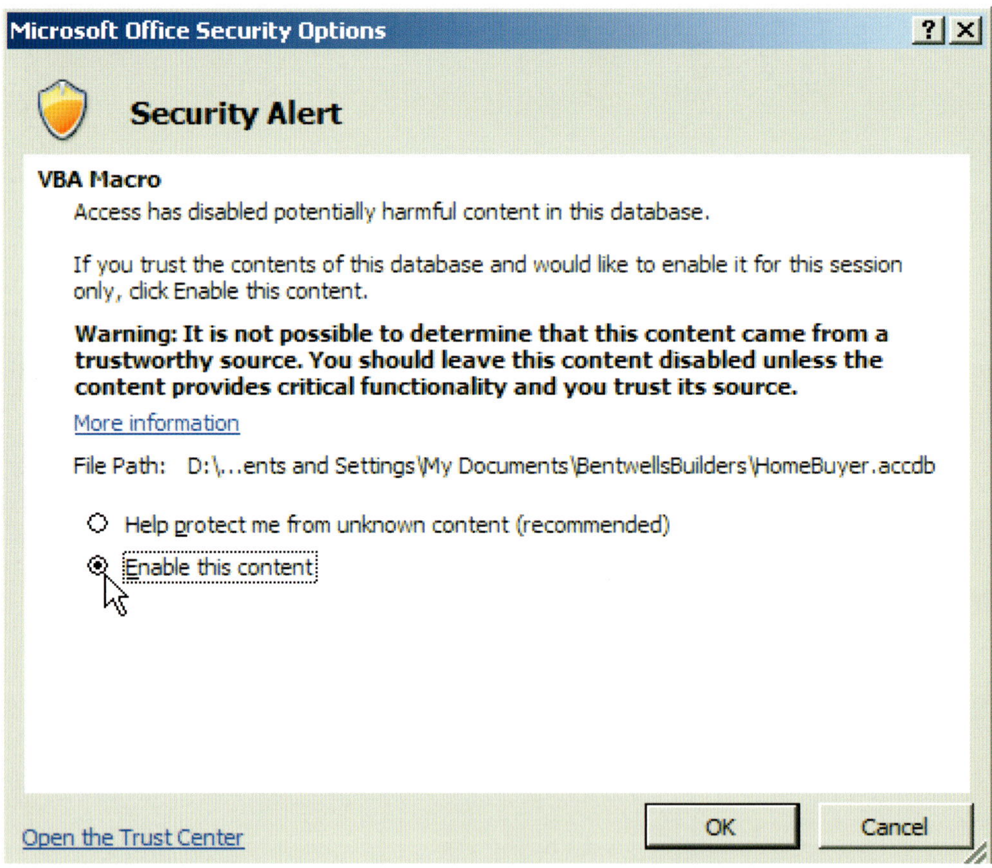

FIgure 3.3

- Double click the **database table** icon just to the left of the database name in the left-hand (**Navigator**) panel.

The database table is displayed on the screen in **Datasheet View**; see Figure 3.4.

Table views

There are two 'views' to choose from when making changes to your database:

- **Design View** is used for making changes to the database **structure**, for example adding a field or changing a field name. This is the view that you used in the last chapter to set up the database structure of the **HomeBuyer** database.
- **Datasheet View** is used for entering and editing the data held in the database. In this chapter we will be using **Datasheet View** to enter information about the customers into the **tblCustomer** table.

Entering data

The table in **Datasheet View** is shown in Figure 3.4.

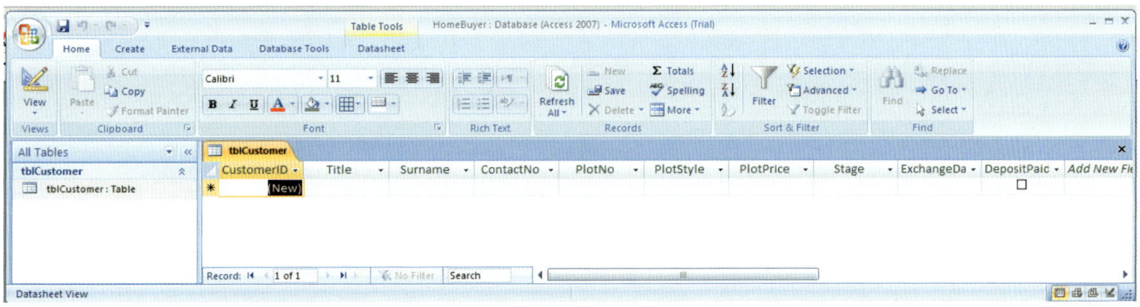

Figure 3.4

- You can make more room in the database window by closing the Navigation pane, click the **Shutter Bar Open/Close Button** (see Figure 3.5).

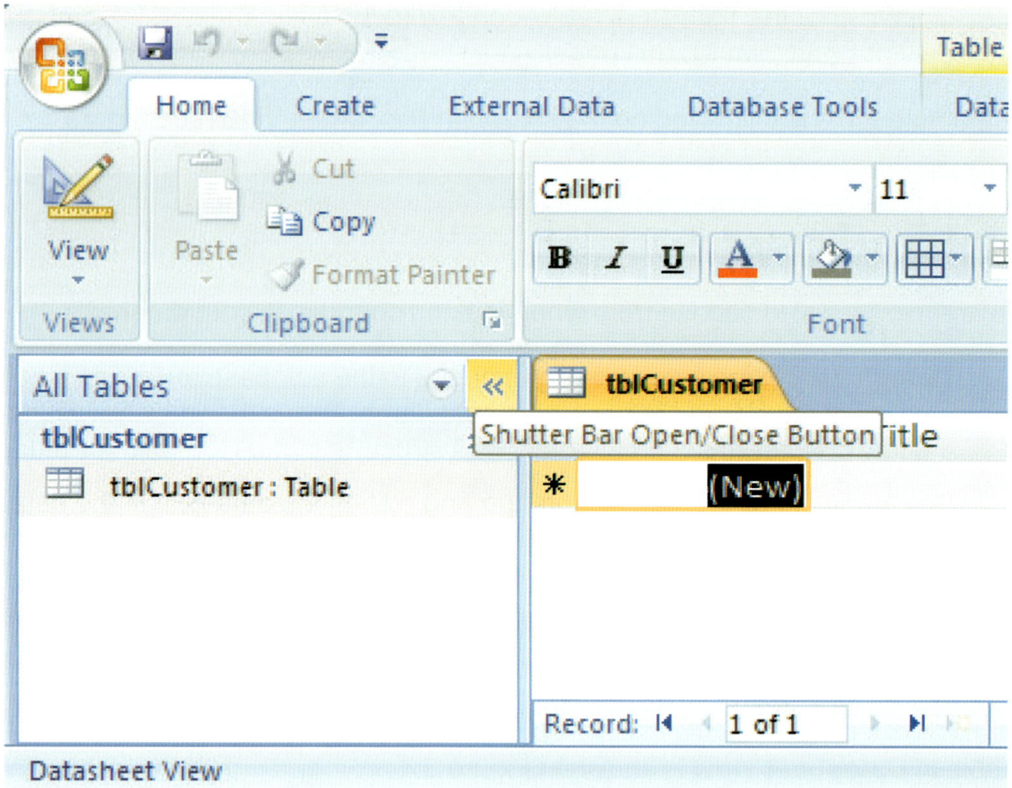

Figure 3.5

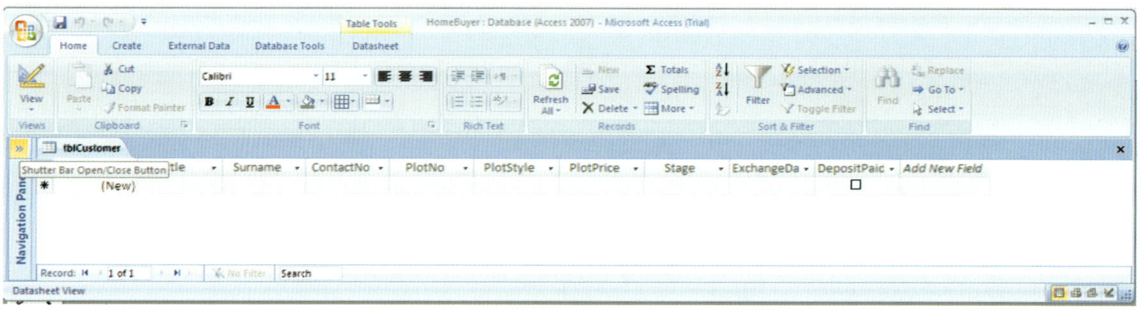

Figure 3.6

Tip:
You can also alter the width of the fields (columns in the table) by clicking between the field names (column headings) and dragging. Obviously this will also affect what of your database table is visible in the database window. You need to be pretty accurate with your mouse pointer when doing this, so some practice is needed!

- Click in the first row of the **CustomerID** column, where it says **(AutoNumber)**. Access will later automatically put a value in here, so you don't have to enter anything.
- Click the **Tab** key to move to the next field, or just click in the next field with the mouse.
- Enter the title **Mr**.
- Go to the **Surname** field and type **Hainsworth**.
- Go to **ContactNo** and type **01474 678456**.
- Go to **PlotNo** and enter **5**.
- Enter **Harrington** as the plot style.

- Enter **185000** as the plot price (Access will add the £ sign because of the data type you set in Design View, and may have delusions of accuracy and add zeros for the pence).
- Enter **Interested** as the stage.
- Leave the **ExchangeDate** field blank – there is no exchange date because the customer has not yet decided to purchase the property.
- Leave **DepositPaid** as **No** (unchecked).

Your table should now look like the one below.

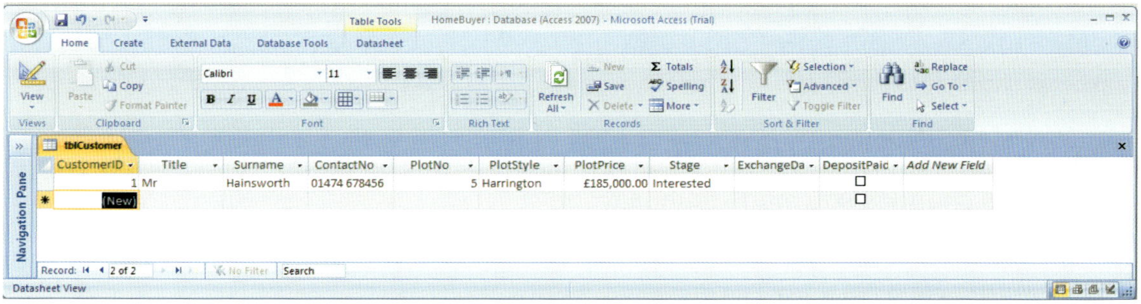

Figure 3.7

Tip:
Hold down Ctrl and press ' in a field to insert the same text or value as in the field above.

- Now enter the rest of the data from the table shown below. Remember that **CustomerID** will be added automatically by Access.

Title	Surname	ContactNo	PlotNo	PlotStyle	PlotPrice	Stage	ExchangeDate	DepositPaid
Mr	Hainsworth	01474 678456	5	Harrington	£185000	Interested		N
Mr	Hodson	01474 212394	1	Kenning	£165000	Interested		N
Mr	Stevenson	01474 665498	3	Scott	£210000	Reserved	1/12/2007	Y
Miss	Hart	01474 374509	5	Harrington	£185000	Interested		N
Mr	Ellis	01474 151884	2	Winnel	£145000	Exchanged	15/08/2007	Y
Mrs	Harris	01474 908635	4	Hamilton	£250000	Reserved	3/12/2007	Y

Table 3.1

- When you have entered all the data, click the **Close** icon in the top right-hand corner of the current window. (Be careful to close just the table window, not Access.)

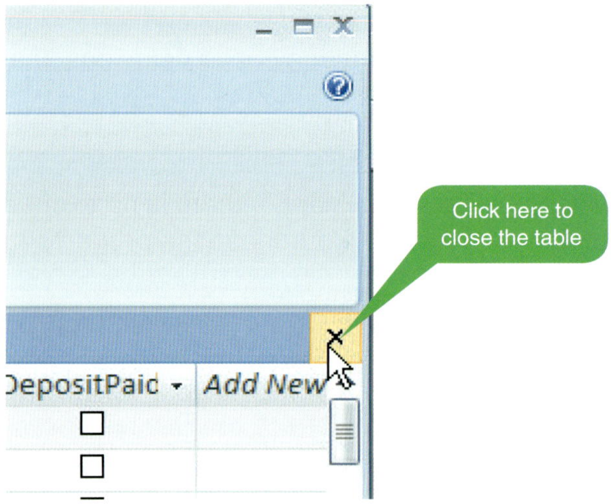

Figure 3.8

- If you have changed the column widths, you will be asked if you want to save the changes you made to the layout.

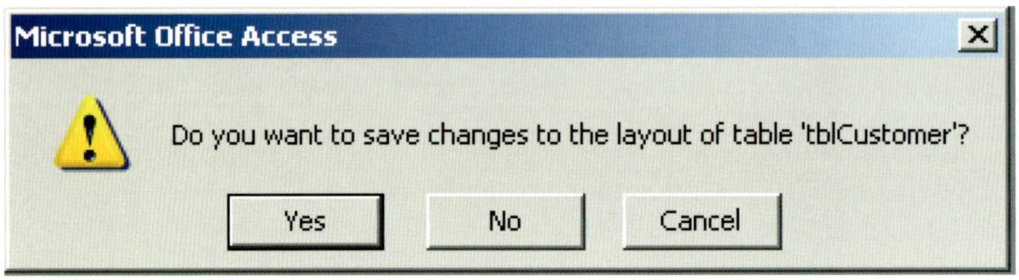

Figure 3.9

- Click **Yes**. You will be returned to the Database window.

Finding, editing and deleting data in a table

- In the Database window, make sure that the Navigation pane is open by clicking the **Shutter Bar Open/Close Button** (see Figures 3.4 and 3.5).
- Double click the icon to the left of the table name. This opens the table in **Datasheet View**. (If you wanted to change the structure of the table, you would need to switch to **Design View** using the **View** button on the **Home** tab of the Ribbon, or right clicking the **table** icon before you open the table and then selecting **Design View** from the shortcut menu.)

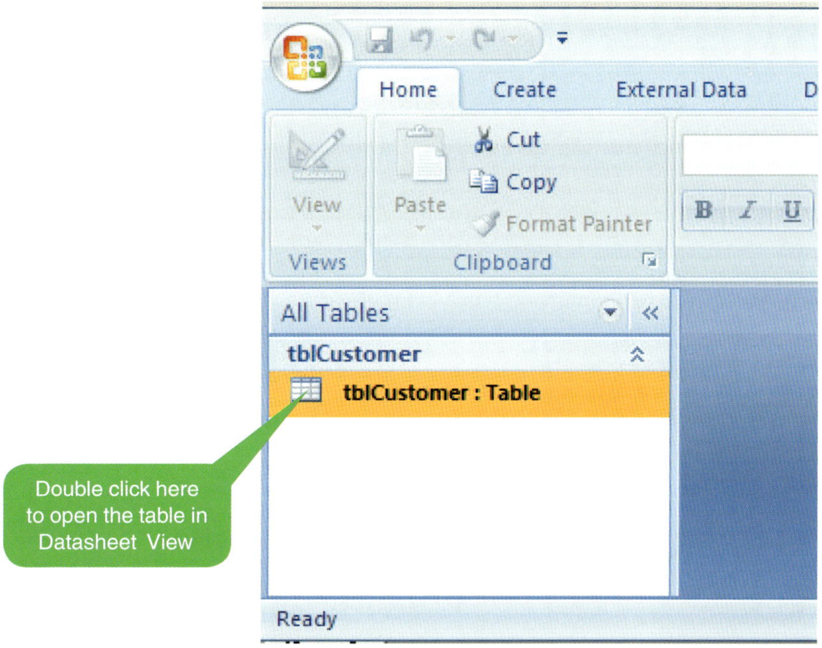

Figure 3.10

The table appears as shown below.

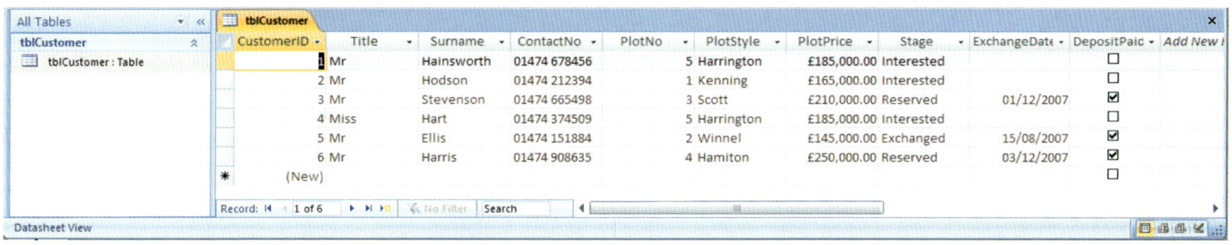

CustomerID	Title	Surname	ContactNo	PlotNo	PlotStyle	PlotPrice	Stage	ExchangeDate	DepositPaid
1	Mr	Hainsworth	01474 678456	5	Harrington	£185,000.00	Interested		☐
2	Mr	Hodson	01474 212394	1	Kenning	£165,000.00	Interested		☐
3	Mr	Stevenson	01474 665498	3	Scott	£210,000.00	Reserved	01/12/2007	☑
4	Miss	Hart	01474 374509	5	Harrington	£185,000.00	Interested		☐
5	Mr	Ellis	01474 151884	2	Winnel	£145,000.00	Exchanged	15/08/2007	☑
6	Mr	Harris	01474 908635	4	Hamiton	£250,000.00	Reserved	03/12/2007	☑
(New)									☐

Figure 3.11

Using the record selectors

You can move to the next or previous record using the record selectors in **Datasheet View**. You can also move to the first or last record, or to a new record at the end of the database. Of course with so few records in the database it is quite easy simply to click in the required row, but you must remember that real databases usually have hundreds or thousands of records, so you may need these techniques one day.

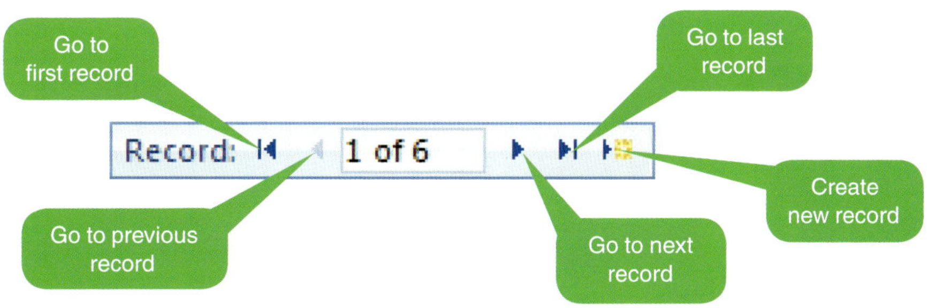

Figure 3.12

Finding a record

Sometimes you may want to find the record for a particular customer. Again, this is most useful on a much larger database.

- Click the mouse anywhere in the **Surname** column, except in Mr Hodson's record.

Suppose you want to find the record for Mr Hodson.

- Click the **Find** icon on the **Home** tab of the **Ribbon**.
- Type the name **Hodson** in the dialogue box, and click **Find Next**.

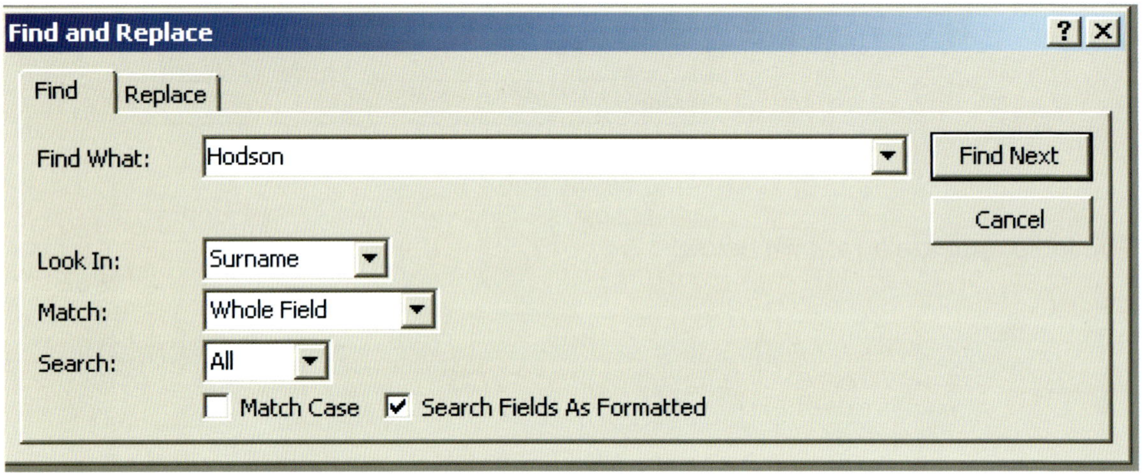

FIgure 3.13

Mr Hodson's record should now be highlighted.

- You can use wildcards such as * in a search. Try searching for **H***. This will find the next record starting with **H** each time you click **Find Next**.
- Close the **Find and Replace** window by clicking its **Close** icon or **Cancel** button.

Editing data

You can change the contents of any field (except **CustomerID** which, being an **Auto-Number** field, is set by Access). You do this by clicking in the field and editing in the normal way. Use the **Backspace** or **Delete** key to delete unwanted text and type the corrections.

Remember you can undo changes using the **Undo** icon.

Tip:
The data in the Primary key is in data type AutoNumber, which is incremented automatically by Access as you add a new record. If you delete a record, although the data for the record disappears, Access retains the original number and will not release it for use in another record of the same table. This results in missing numbers in the datasheet view of the table – each missing number indicates the position of a deleted record.

Adding a new record

Suppose a new customer has registered an interest in a property, and their details have to be added to the HomeBuyer database. Their details are shown below:

Title	Surname	ContactNo	PlotNo	PlotStyle	PlotPrice	Stage	ExchangeDate	DepositPaid
Mr	Fairbairn	01474 472967	1	Kenning	£165000	Interested		N

Table 3.2

There are two ways to add a new record:

- either click in the next blank line
- or click the **New Record** icon on either the record selector (see Figure 3.12) or the **Menu bar**.
- Enter Mr Fairbairn's details from the table above.

The first method is easy for such a small database, but if there were hundreds of customers in the database you wouldn't want to scroll down to an empty row. For larger databases you would use the **New Record** icon.

Deleting a record

To delete Mr Fairbairn's record:

- Click the **Record Selector** for Mr Fairbairn's record.
- Click the **Delete** button on the **Home** tab in the **Records** group of the **Ribbon**. You will see a message:

Figure 3.14

- Click **Yes** to delete the record.

If you have added or changed any other records, restore them now to how they are in Table 3.1. It does not matter if the **CustomerID** field is different in your records (which can be the case if you have deleted any records: see previous Tip).

- Save your table.
- Close the database unless you plan to carry on now to Chapter 4!

Chapter 4 – Data Validation

It is important to make sure that you have entered the correct data into the database. If you make a mistake entering data, especially in very large databases, the error can be very difficult to trace. For example, if you entered *Interest* instead of *Interested* as the stage for a customer, then when you searched the database for all those who were interested in a particular plot, that particular customer wouldn't be shown.

Although there are many errors that the database cannot detect (such as a misspelt name), there are many that it can.

You can write a set of rules which the data must abide by. For example:

- There are only 30 plots, therefore **PlotNo** must be between 1 and 30.
- Only **Interested, Reserved, Exchanged** or **Completed** can be entered in the **Stage** field.
- The **Surname** field cannot be left blank.

The process of checking that the data meets various 'rules' is called **validation**. The rules themselves are called **validation rules**.

Alongside each rule, you can enter some text that Access will show to the user if they enter invalid data. This is called **validation text**.

Types of rule

There are various types of rule that you can enter, and they are listed in the table below.

Operator	Meaning	Example
<	less than	<20
<=	less than or equal to	<=20
>	greater than	>0
>=	greater than or equal to	>=0
=	equal to	=20 ="Harrington" OR "Kenning"
<>	not equal to	<>"Kenning"
BETWEEN	test for a range of values. Must be two comparison values (a low and high value) separated by AND operator	BETWEEN 01/12/2007 AND 25/12/2007

Table 4.1

- Click the **Options** button, as before and then click **Open the Trust Centre**.
- Select **Trusted Locations** and click **Allow Trusted Locations on my network** (ignoring the dire warning), then click **Add new location**.
- In the **Microsoft Office Trusted Location** dialogue box, click **Browse** and navigate to the folder which contains your database. Click **OK** – you should see your new location added to the list; click **OK** and then **OK** again.

Tip:
To avoid having to re-set the security permissions every time you open an existing database, you can proceed as described (left).

Entering the validation rules

- Open the **HomeBuyer** database.
- In the Database window, select **tblCustomer** and right click to obtain the shortcut menu.

- Click **Design View**.

We are going to enter a validation rule for the **PlotNo** field. The rule we will use is: **PlotNo** must be between 1 and 30.

- Click in the **PlotNo** field name.

Notice that there are two rows in the field properties at the bottom of the screen named **Validation Rule** and **Validation Text**. This is where we will enter the rules.

- In the Field Properties, click in the **Validation Rule** row.
- Type **Between 1 and 30** and click **Enter**.
- In the **Validation Text** row type **The Plot Number** must be between 1 and 30 and click **Enter**.

Tip:
You will not see these rows if the cursor is in the CustomerID field. You do not need validation for this field because it is an AutoNumber field.

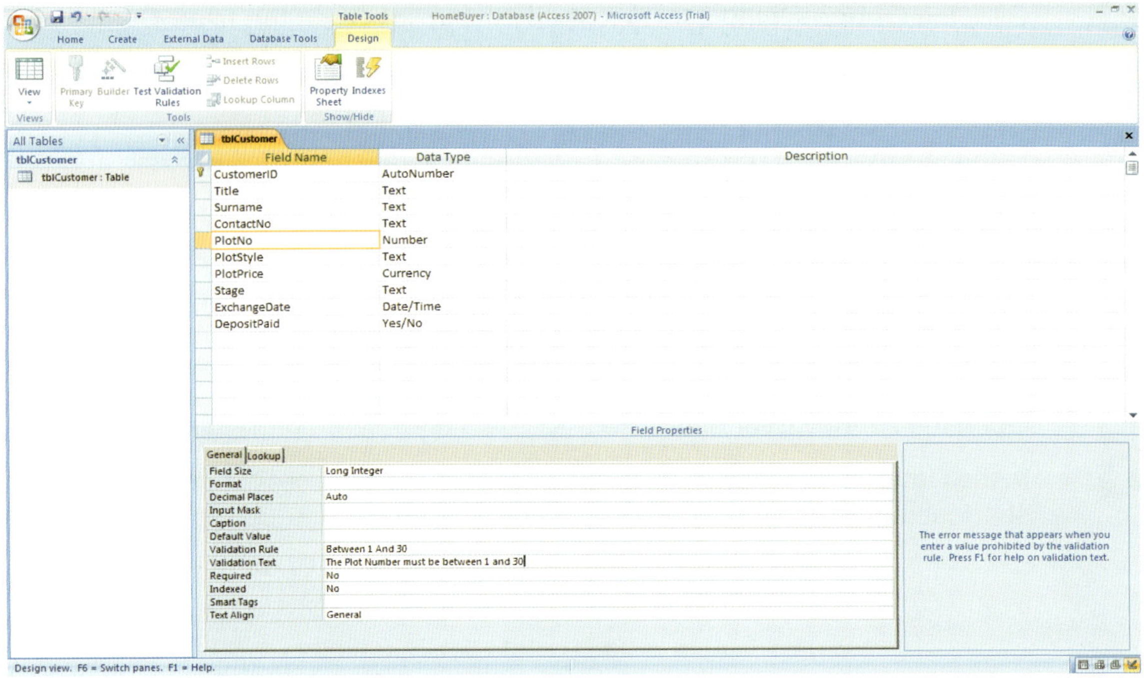

Figure 4.1

Return to **Datasheet View** by clicking the **View** button on the **Table Tools Design** tab of the **Ribbon**.

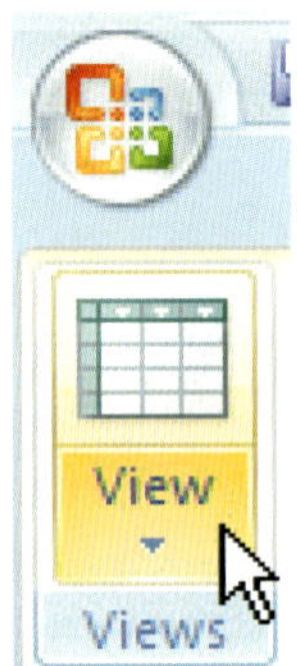

You will be asked to save the changes you have just made. Click **Yes**,

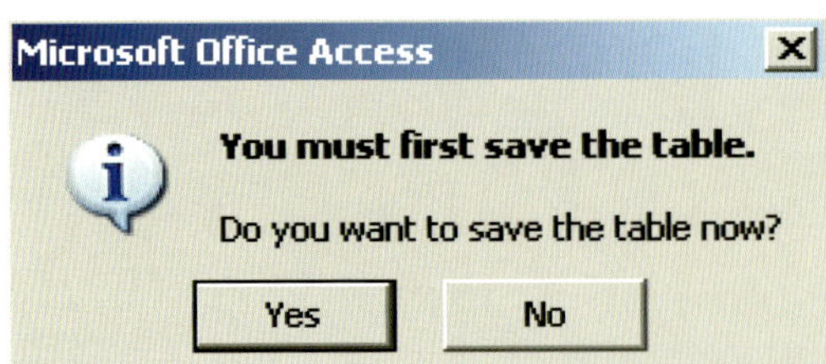

Figure 4.2

and **Yes** to the prompt about data integrity rules; see Figure 4.3:

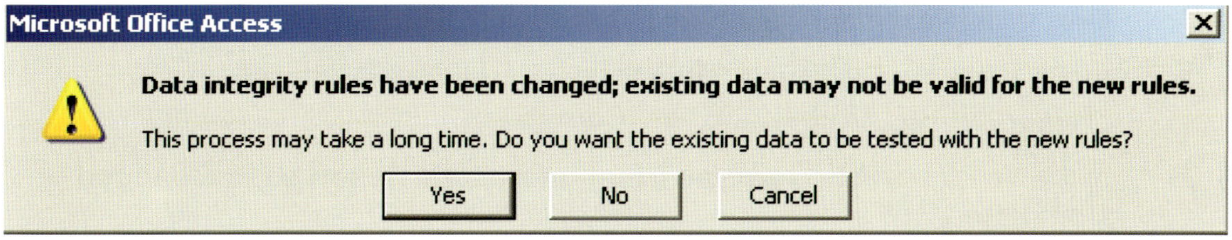

Figure 4.3

The warning is given because there is data entered in the table already (the plot numbers) and Access is worried that this existing data may not fit the new Validation Rule.

Test the validation rule

We will test the rule by entering a new record that does not obey the validation rule.

Title	Surname	ContactNo	PlotNo	PlotStyle	PlotPrice	Stage	ExchangeDate	DepositPaid
Mrs	Lock	01474 505783	41	Kenning	£165000	Interested		N

Table 4.2

- Click in the empty row below Mrs Harris's record and enter the **Title** as **Mrs**.
- Enter the **Surname** and **ContactNo** for Mrs Lock as they appear in the table above.
- Enter the **PlotNo** as **41** and click **Enter**.

Tip:
Access will not allow you to exit the field until the value in that field obeys the validation rule. You can click OK in the Warning box and then press Esc (keyboard) to abandon the data in the PlotNo field.

A message will appear on the screen displaying the Validation Text that you entered:

Figure 4.4

- Change the **PlotNo** to **1** and click **Enter**.
- Now enter the other details for **Mrs Lock** from the table above.

Setting the other validation rules

Now we will set the rule for the **Stage** field. The rule we will use is: the stage must be one of **Interested, Reserved, Exchanged** or **Completed**.

- Return to **Design View** by clicking the **Design View** icon.

Click in the field name for **Stage** to bring up its field properties.

In the **Validation Rule** row of the field properties type **= "Interested" or "Reserved" or "Exchanged" or "Completed"**.

In the **Validation Text** row type **Enter Interested, Reserved, Exchanged or Completed**.

More testing

Return to **Datasheet View** by clicking the **Datasheet View** icon.

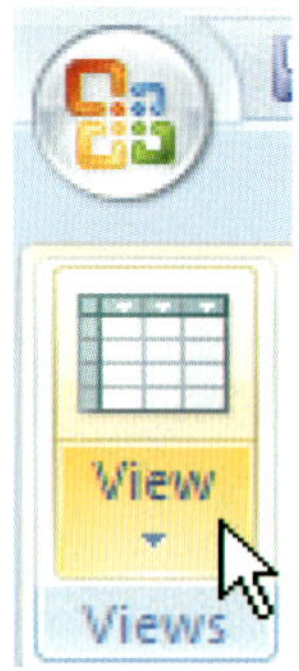

Click **Yes** to save the changes and **Yes** to the prompt about data integrity rules.

In the table below are more records that have to be entered.

Try entering invalid values for **PlotNo** and **Stage**. You should see your error messages appearing.

Tip:
Always test your validation rules by trying to enter invalid data. You can press Esc to cancel the invalid data without saving it. Pressing Esc twice deletes the whole record.

Title	Surname	ContactNo	PlotNo	PlotStyle	PlotPrice	Stage	ExchangeDate	DepositPaid
Mr	Iqbal	01474 673028	6	Kenning	£165000	Reserved	7/12/2002	Y
Miss	Jones	01474 255836	1	Kenning	£165000	Interested		N
Mr	Harris	01474 682453	5	Harrington	£185000	Reserved	5/1/2003	Y

Table 4.3

When you have entered the records with the data shown, save and close your table.

Close Access if this is the end of a session.

Chapter 5 – Sorting, Formatting and Printing Tables

In Chapter 7 you will learn how to create formatted reports. Sometimes, however, it is useful just to be able to sort and print the contents of a table. You can print all the fields, or just some of them.

- Open the **HomeBuyer** database.
- Double click **tblCustomer** to open it.

Tip:
Remember you can open your table in datasheet view by clicking Open in the Database window.

Sorting records

You can perform a simple sort on one field by clicking anywhere in the column you want to sort on and clicking one of the two **Sort** buttons (**Sort Ascending** and **Sort Descending**) on the **Table Tool Home** tab of the Ribbon.

Figure 5.1

To sort the customers in the table by surname:

- Click in the **Surname** field and click the **Sort Ascending** button. The records will now be sorted in ascending order of surname, as shown below. Notice the additional icon in the field heading 'Surname' to indicate the field is sorted in ascending order.

CustomerID	Title	Surname	ContactNo	PlotNo	PlotStyle	PlotPrice	Stage	ExchangeDate	DepositPaid	Add New Field
5	Mr	Ellis	01474 151884	2	Winnel	£145,000.00	Exchanged	15/08/2007	☑	
1	Mr	Hainsworth	01474 678456	5	Harrington	£185,000.00	Interested		☐	
10	Mr	Harris	01474 682453	5	Harrington	£185,000.00	Reserved	05/01/2008	☑	
6	Mrs	Harris	01474 908635	4	Hamiton	£250,000.00	Reserved	03/12/2007	☑	
4	Miss	Hart	01474 374509	5	Harrington	£185,000.00	Interested		☐	
2	Mr	Hodson	01474 212394	1	Kenning	£165,000.00	Interested		☐	
8	Mr	Iqbal	01474 673028	6	Kenning	£165,000.00	Reserved	07/12/2007	☑	
9	Miss	Jones	01474 255836	1	Kenning	£165,000.00	Interested		☐	
7	Mrs	Lock	01474 505783	1	Kenning	£165,000.00	Interested		☐	
3	Mr	Stevenson	01474 665498	3	Scott	£210,000.00	Reserved	01/12/2007	☑	
(New)									☐	

Figure 5.2

Formatting and printing a datasheet

You can print a datasheet just as it is, or you can format it first by hiding unwanted columns, changing the order of the columns and changing column widths. We will practise these techniques.

With **tblCustomer** open in **Datasheet View**, click the **Office Button** and select **Print** and then **Print Preview**.

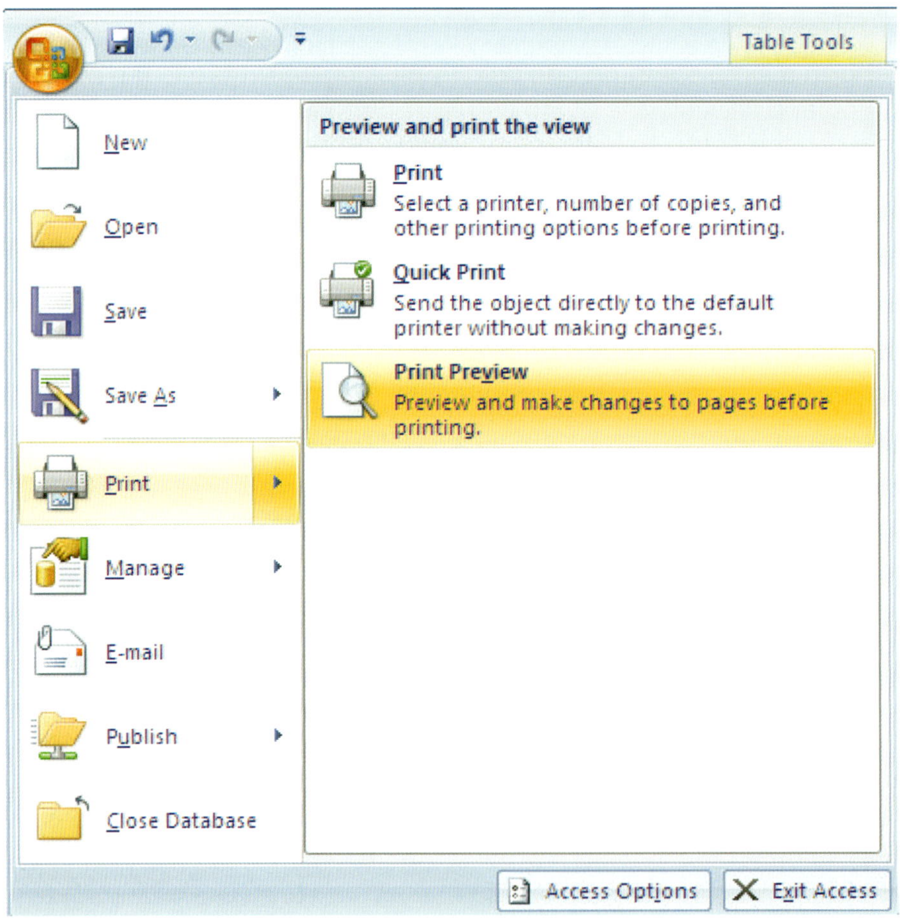

Figure 5.3

Your data appears as shown below:

Tip:
If it's too small to read, click on it.

CustomerID	Title	Surname	ContactNo	PlotNo	PlotStyle
5	Mr	Ellis	01474 151884	2	Winnel
1	Mr	Hainsworth	01474 678456	5	Harrington
10	Mr	Harris	01474 682453	5	Harrington
6	Mrs	Harris	01474 908635	4	Hamilton
4	Miss	Hart	01474 374509	5	Harrington
2	Mr	Hodson	01474 212394	1	Kenning
8	Mr	Iqbal	01474 673028	6	Kenning
9	Miss	Jones	01474 255836	1	Kenning
7	Mrs	Lock	01474 505783	1	Kenning
3	Mr	Stevenson	01474 665498	3	Scott

Figure 5.4

The whole datasheet may not fit on one page in **Portrait view**. You can use the page selector at the bottom of the screen to view the second page.

The **Print Preview** toolbar appears at the top of the screen. You can **Zoom** in on a page by clicking anywhere on it, or by clicking the **Zoom** icon.

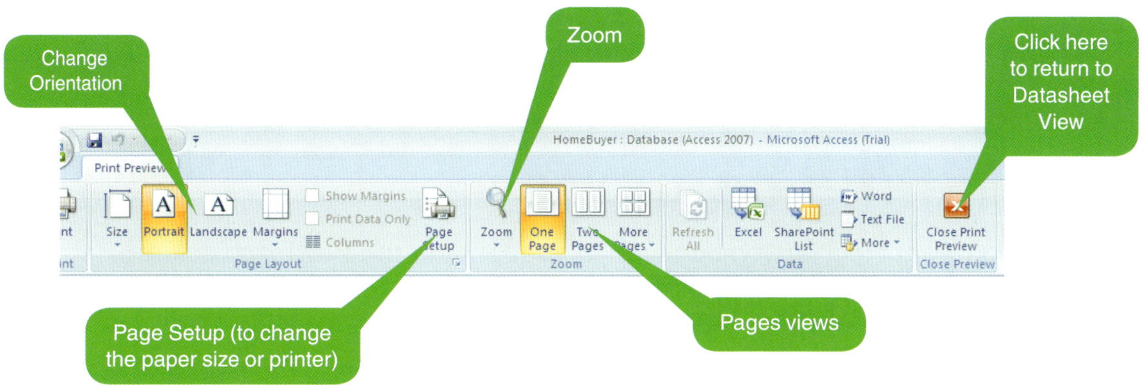

Figure 5.5

Changing the page layout

Using the **Page Layout** controls you can change the page layout to **Landscape** view.

- Click the **Landscape** button. If the table didn't fit on one page before, it should now.
- Click the **Close Print Preview** button to return to **Datasheet View**.

Hiding and Unhiding columns

Sometimes you may not want to print all the columns in the datasheet. You can hide the columns that you don't want.

- Make sure you have **tblCustomer** open in **Datasheet View**.
- Drag across the column headers **ExchangeDate** and **DepositPaid**.
- Right click within the highlighted columns and select **Hide Columns** from the shortcut menu. The columns will be hidden.
- To unhide the columns, you right click in any of the field headings of the table and then select **Unhide Columns** from the shortcut menu; the **Unhide**

Columns dialogue box appears. Click (i.e. tick) the boxes of the columns (fields) that you wish to reappear; see Figure 5.6:

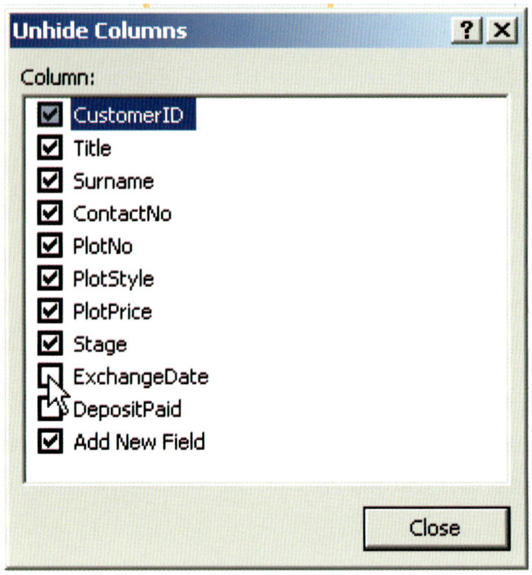

Figure 5.6

Formatting columns

Suppose you want the **PlotStyle** column to appear after the **PlotPrice** column.

- Click the **PlotStyle** column header to select the whole column (field).
- Click again and hold down the mouse button, then drag the header to between the **PlotPrice** column and the **Stage** column.
- Adjust the column widths by double clicking in the column header on the border between each column.

Your table should now appear as shown below.

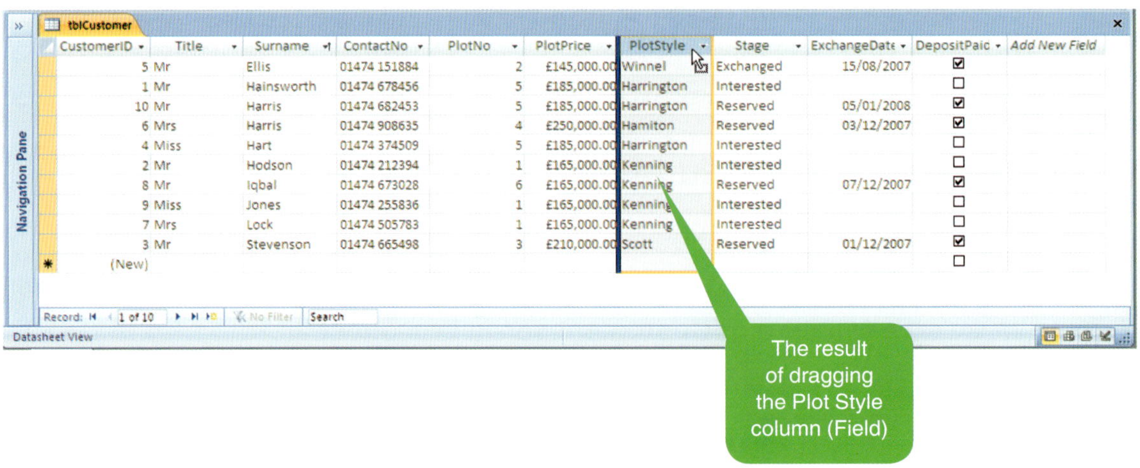

Figure 5.7

Click the **Print Preview** icon again to see what the page will look like when printed out.

Click the **Office** button, click **Save** and then click the **Office** button again and select **Close Database**.

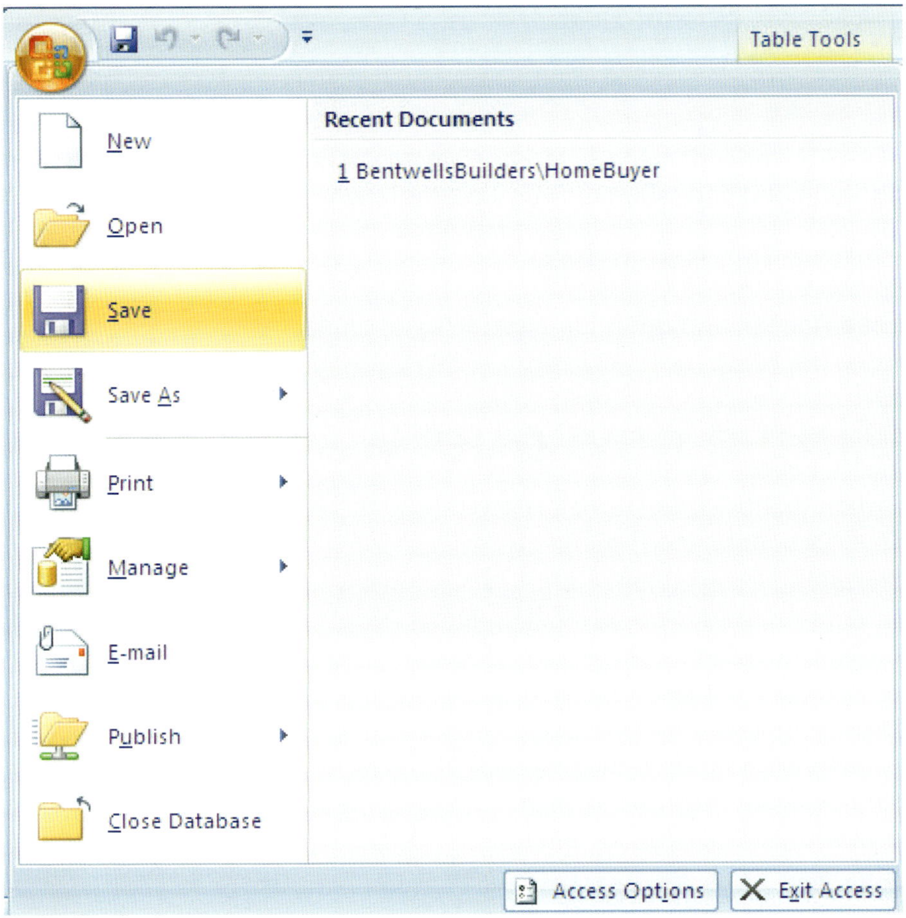

Figure 5.8

Finally, after the database has closed, close Access by clicking the cross at the top right of the screen; see Figure 5.9.

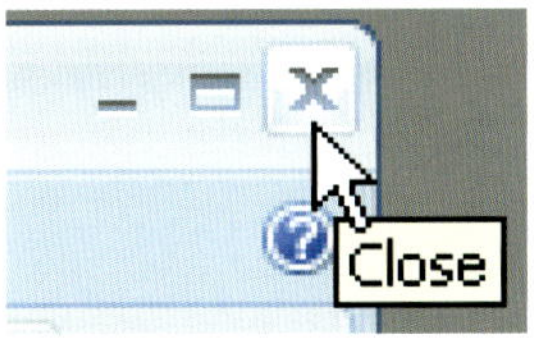

Figure 5.9

Chapter 6 – Making Queries

One of the most useful things you can do with a database is to find all the records that satisfy a certain condition, such as “All customers who are interested in plot 5”.

This is called **querying the database**.

- Load Access and open the **HomeBuyer** database table.

Creating a new query

- Switch to the **Table Tools Create** tab on the **Ribbon** and click the **Query Design** button; see Figure 6.1.

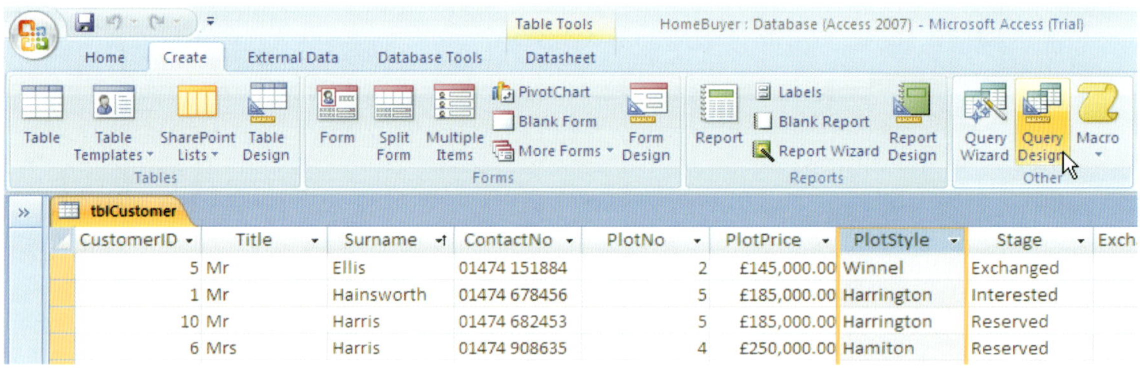

Figure 6.1

- The **Query Design View** window opens with the **Show Table** dialogue box; in this case there is just a table, **tblCustomer**.

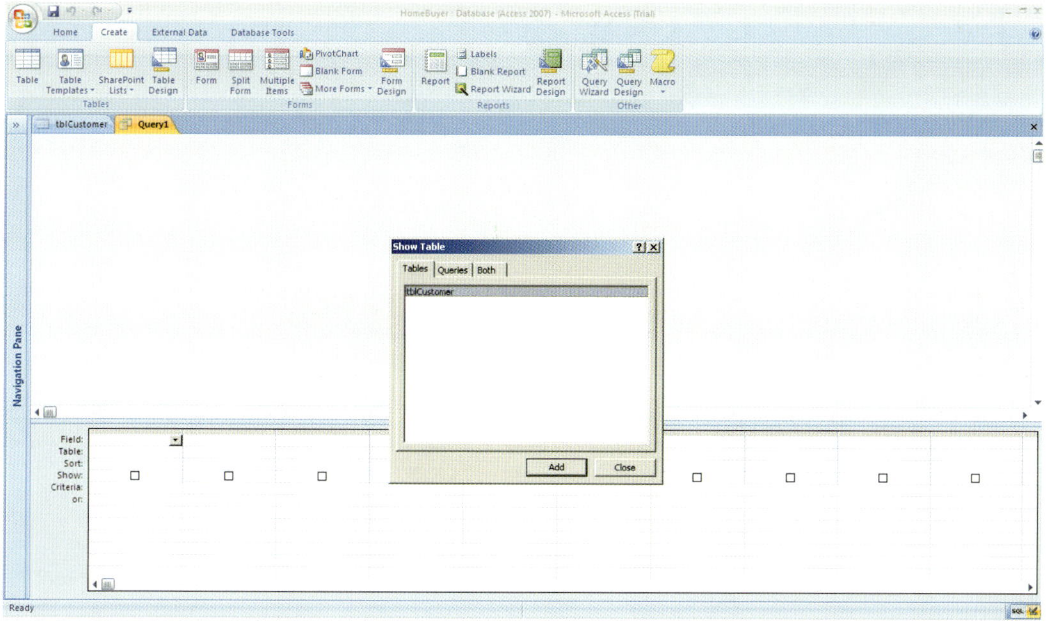

Figure 6.2

In the **Show Table** dialogue box, click **Add** to add **tblCustomer** to the **Query** window and then click **Close**.

Figure 6.3

Selecting fields to appear in the query

The top half of the **Query Design** window shows the table that you just added in the **Show Table** window. The bottom half contains the **query grid**. You need to place selected fields onto the grid from the **tblCustomer** table. These will be fields that you want to display, or for which you want to specify conditions, called **criteria**.

In the **tblCustomer** pane in the upper half of the window, double click in turn the fields **Title**, **Surname**, **ContactNo**, **PlotNo**, **Stage** and **ExchangeDate**. As you double-click the fields, they will be placed in the query grid.

Tip:
To place a field in the query grid you can either double click the field in the tblCustomer pane, or drag it onto the query grid.

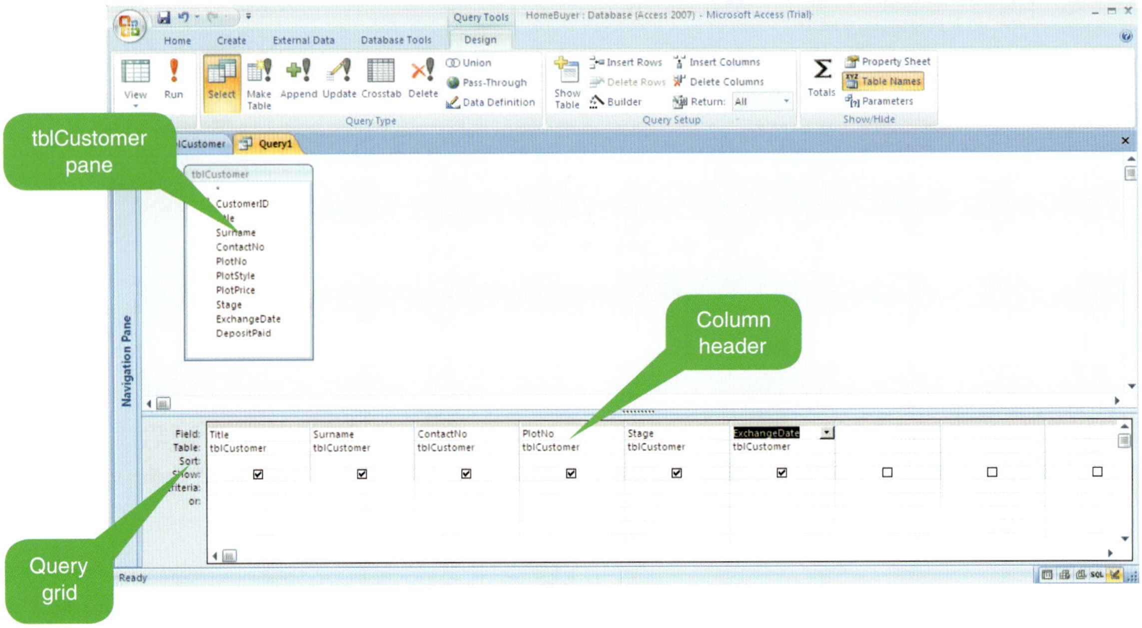

Figure 6.4

Suppose you now change your mind and want to delete the **ExchangeDate** field from the query.

- Click in the column header of the **ExchangeDate** field to select the column and click the **Delete Columns** button on the **Query Tools Design** tab. Be careful to avoid using the **Delete** button on the same tab, which uses the query to delete data in the table.

To add the **PlotStyle** field to your query:

- Click and drag **PlotStyle** from the **tblCustomer** pane and put it on top of the next blank column on the right. It will be inserted in that position. (You could have double-clicked the field name to do the same thing.)

Setting simple criteria

Now suppose you want to find all the customers who are interested in Plot 5.

- In the **Criteria** row of the **PlotNo** column, enter 5.
- Now run your query to see the results. Click either the **Run** or **View** button on the toolbar.

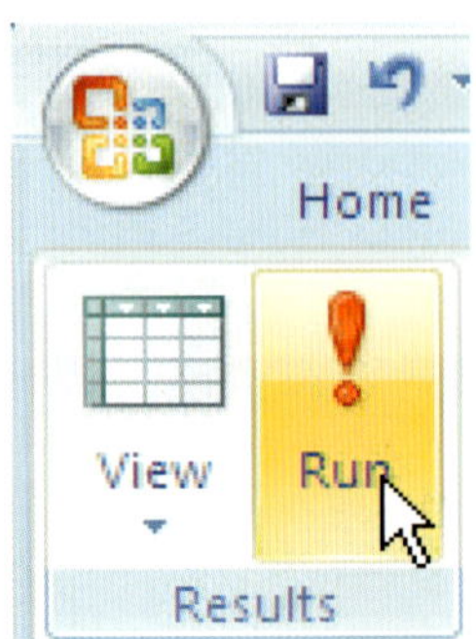

The results appear as shown below.

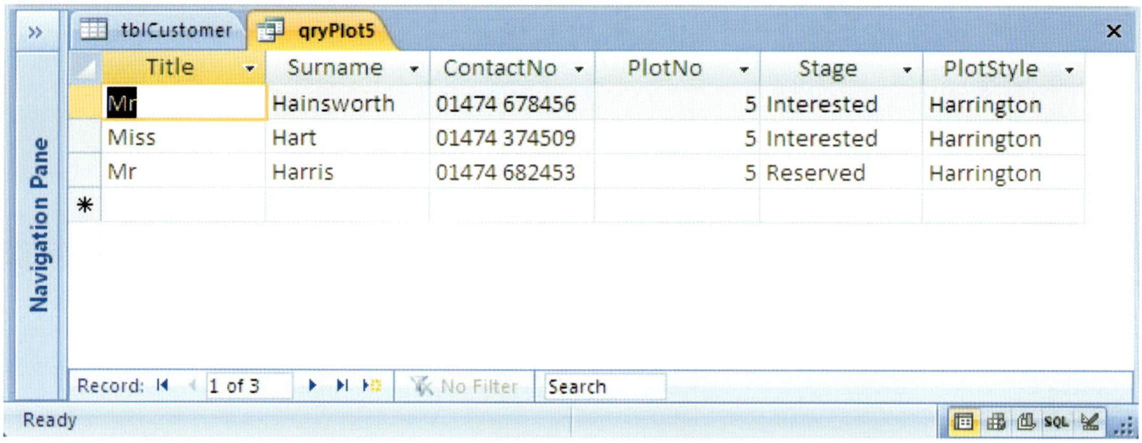

Figure 6.5

Saving a query

You can save a query so that it can be run whenever you like. For example, after you have added more records to the database, you may want to search it again for customers interested in Plot 5.

Saving the query saves the **question** not the **answer**.

- Click the **Office** button or right click the **queries** tab and select **save**. The **Save As** dialogue box appears where you can type in a suitable name for the query.
- Save the query as **qryPlot5**.

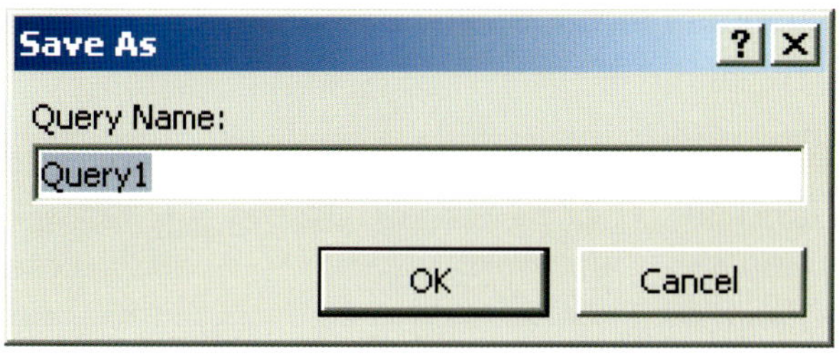

Figure 6.6

Tip:
Using the common naming convention, all queries are saved with a name starting with qry.

Multiple criteria

Suppose you wanted to find all the customers signed up for either Plot 5 or Plot 1. You will notice that the row under **Criteria** is headed **or**.

- Return to **Design View** to change the query.

In the row headed **or**, under the criteria **5**, type **1**.

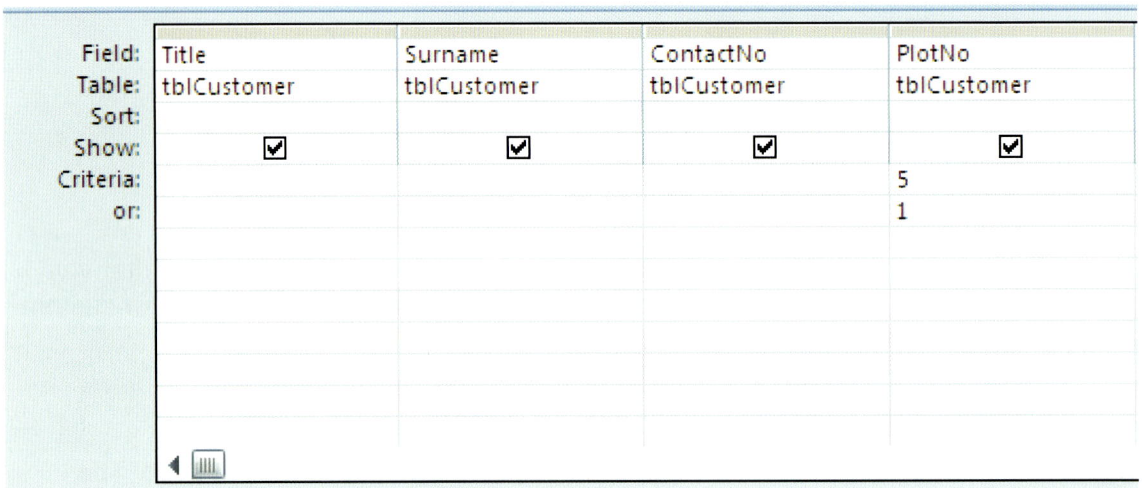

Field:	Title	Surname	ContactNo	PlotNo
Table:	tblCustomer	tblCustomer	tblCustomer	tblCustomer
Sort:				
Show:	☑	☑	☑	☑
Criteria:				5
or:				1

Figure 6.7

Run the query again.

The query results table should now look like this:

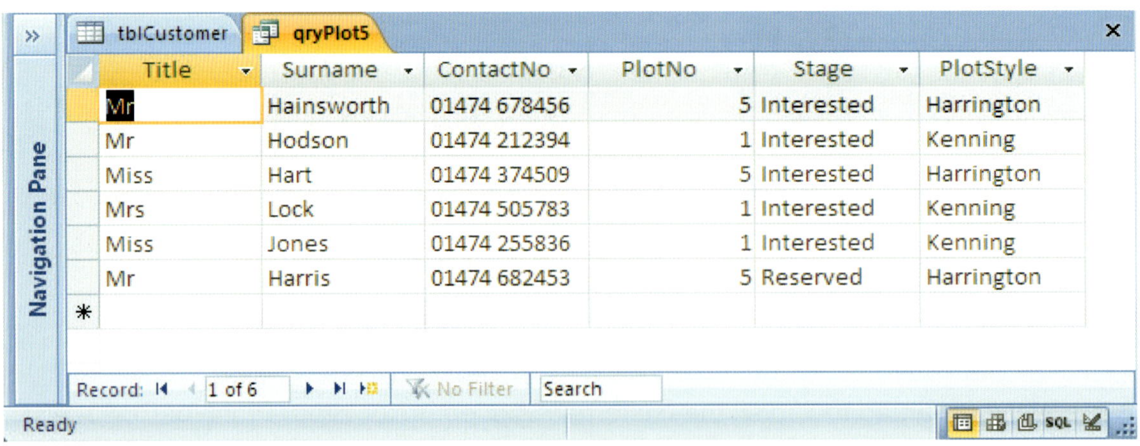

Title	Surname	ContactNo	PlotNo	Stage	PlotStyle
Mr	Hainsworth	01474 678456	5	Interested	Harrington
Mr	Hodson	01474 212394	1	Interested	Kenning
Miss	Hart	01474 374509	5	Interested	Harrington
Mrs	Lock	01474 505783	1	Interested	Kenning
Miss	Jones	01474 255836	1	Interested	Kenning
Mr	Harris	01474 682453	5	Reserved	Harrington

Figure 6.8

Sorting results

It would be nice if the query results were sorted alphabetically by surname.

- Return to **Design View**.
- Under the **Surname** column, select **Ascending** from the **Sort** row; see Figure 6.9.

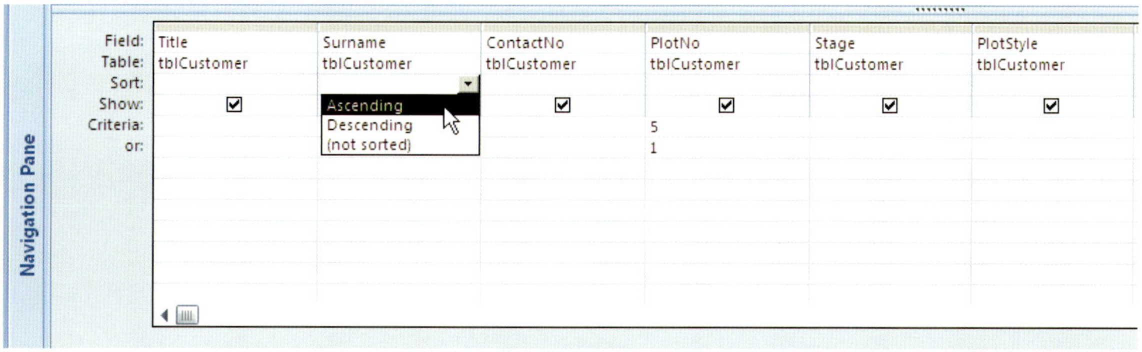

Figure 6.9

- Run the query to see that the results are now sorted by **Surname**.

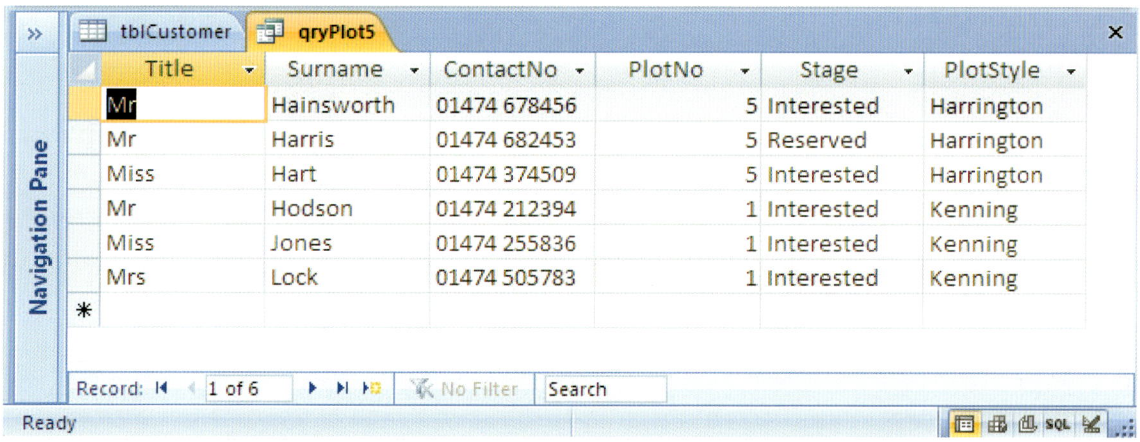

Title	Surname	ContactNo	PlotNo	Stage	PlotStyle
Mr	Hainsworth	01474 678456	5	Interested	Harrington
Mr	Harris	01474 682453	5	Reserved	Harrington
Miss	Hart	01474 374509	5	Interested	Harrington
Mr	Hodson	01474 212394	1	Interested	Kenning
Miss	Jones	01474 255836	1	Interested	Kenning
Mrs	Lock	01474 505783	1	Interested	Kenning

Figure 6.10

If you just click **Save**, then you will save the changes you have made over the top of the original query. To keep the old query as was, before changes were made, you will need to save this query with a different name. Do this:

- Click the **Office** button and select **Save As** and then **Save Object As**; see Figure 6.11.

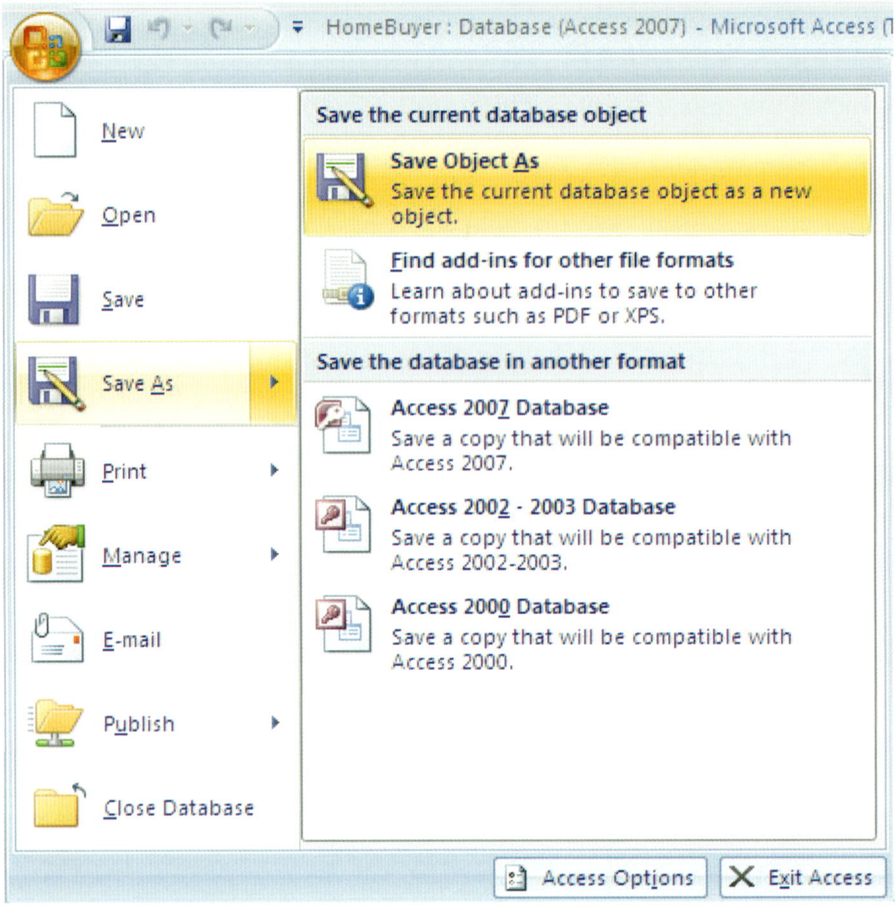

Figure 6.11

In the **Save As** dialogue box type the name of your query as **qryPlot1&Plot5** and click **OK**.

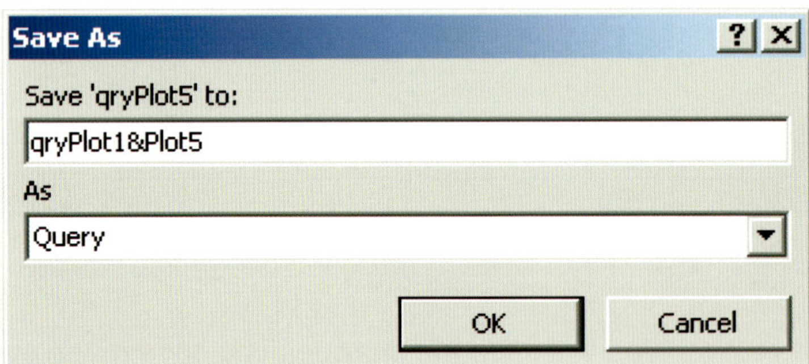

Figure 6.12

Close your query.

Chapter 7 – Presenting Data

Suppose you want to present the data in a table or query in a neater way, for example with a proper title and date. For this you would use a **Report**. Reports allow you to present data in a wide variety of ways. They can be based on queries or on tables.

- Load Access and open the **HomeBuyer** database if it is not already open. It should be in a folder named **BentwellsBuilders**.

Making a report

The sales staff need a report of everyone interested in Plot 5. Remember that you created **qryPlot5** in the last chapter, which contained only those customers who were interested in Plot 5. Our report will be based on this query.

- Switch to the **Create** tab on the **Ribbon** and click the **Report Wizard** button.

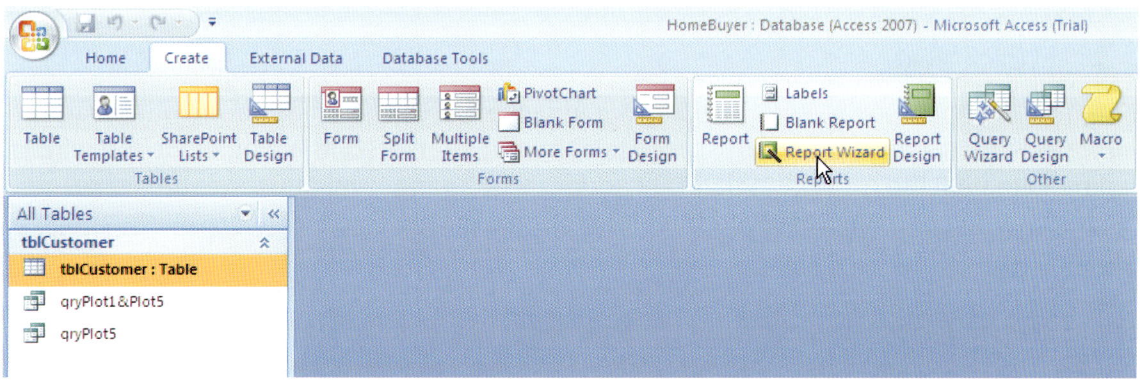

Figure 7.1

- In the **Tables/Queries** drop-down list select **qryPlot5**.

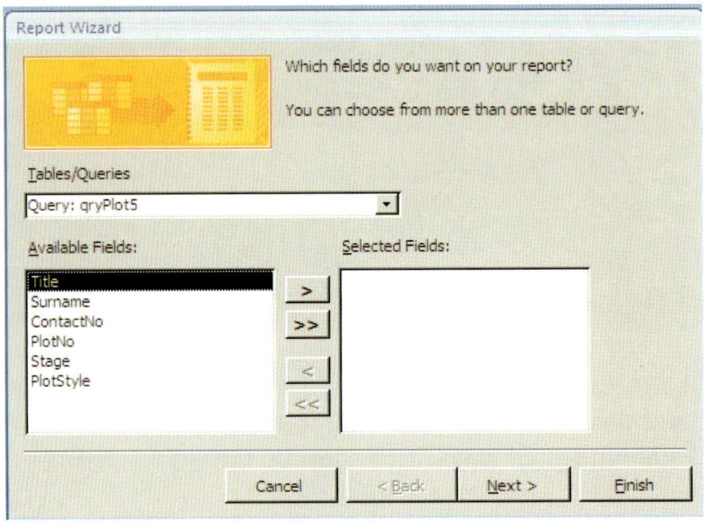

Figure 7.2

- In the **Available Fields** box below will be a list of all the (unhidden) fields in the query. Highlight **Title** and click > to make it appear in the report.

- Repeat this for **Surname, ContactNo** and **Stage**.

We will leave **PlotNo** out of the report because we know that all these customers are interested in Plot 5.

- Click **Next**.

The next dialogue box will ask about grouping levels. Even after someone has reserved a plot the sales staff will keep the records of others interested in a plot, since the sale is not definite until the exchange date. By adding a grouping level of **Stage**, the report will list a customer who has reserved the plot separately from those who are interested in it.

- Click **Stage** so that it is highlighted, then click >.

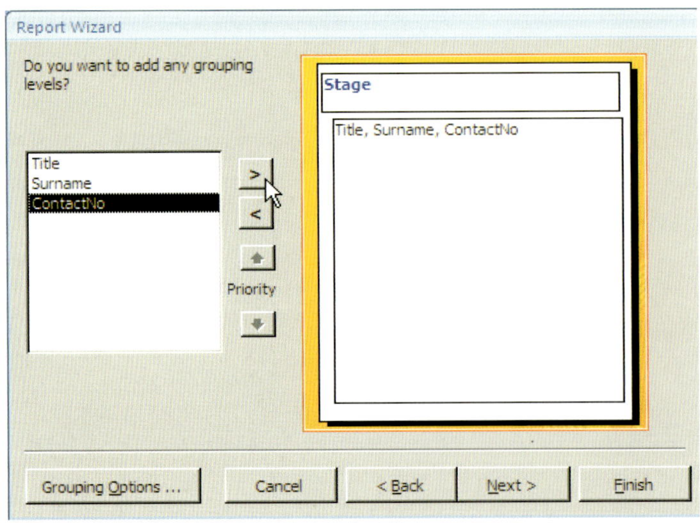

Figure 7.3

Tip:
By default, Access saves the report under the name that you give for the title. The common naming convention is to save reports with a name beginning rpt.

Click **Next**.

Now you are asked for a sort order. We want the customers in **Surname** order.

In the first drop-down list select **Surname** and check that the sort is in **Ascending** order.

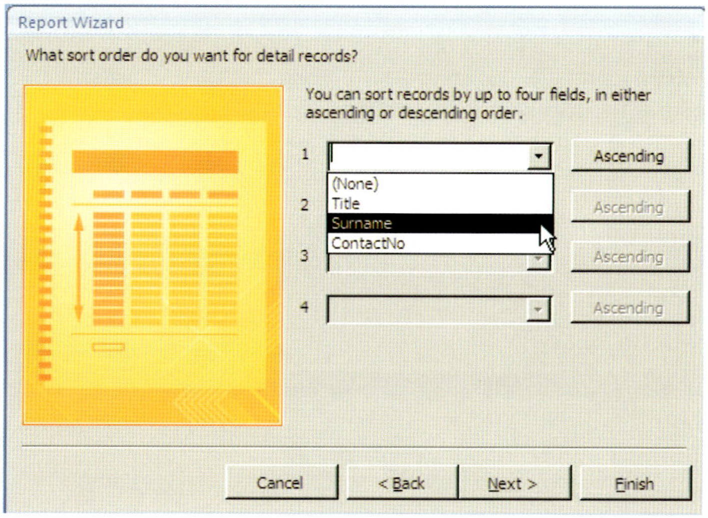

Figure 7.4

The next two dialogue boxes are about the format and style of the report. We will leave these as they are for now.

Click **Next** three more times, until Access asks **What title do you want for your report?**

Enter **rptPlot5** then click **Finish**.

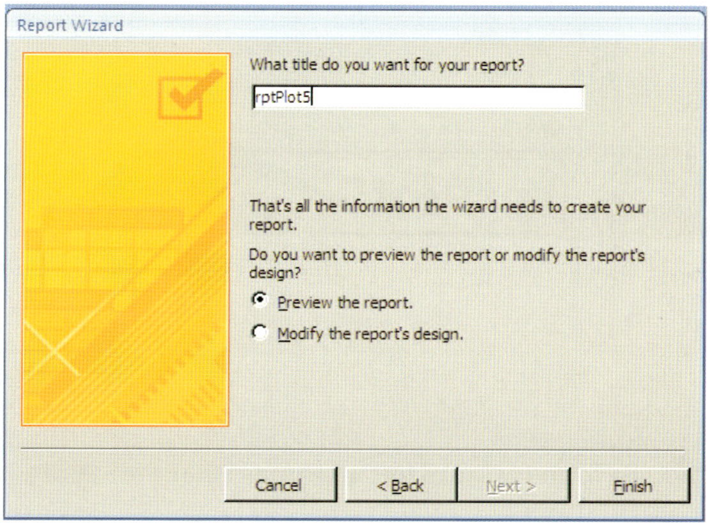

Figure 7.5

The report, saved as **rptPlot5**, should appear as shown in Figure 7.6.

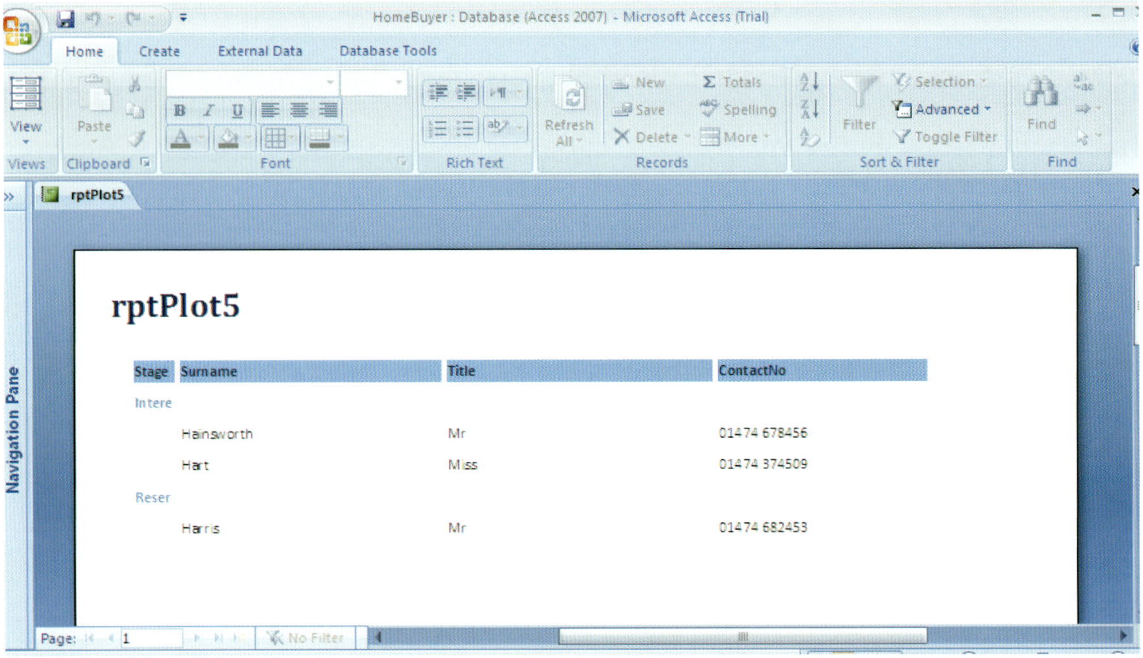

Figure 7.6

Changing the titles

At the moment the title of the report is **rptPlot5**. To change the title to **Customer Sheet for Plot 5**:

- Click **Close Print Preview** to return to **Design View**.
- Click in the box that says **rptPlot5**. Click again and the text cursor should appear in the box.

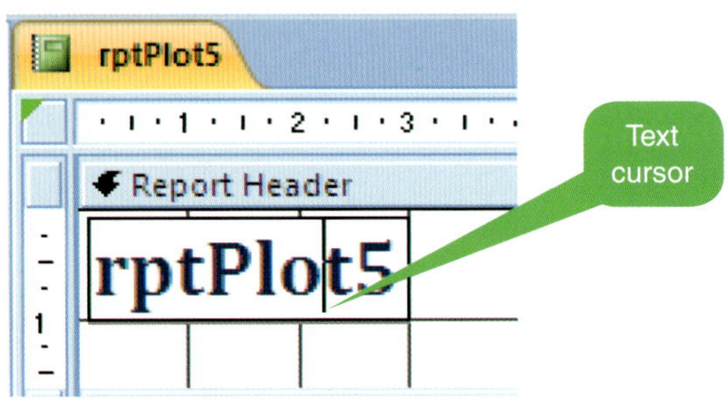

Figure 7.7

You can now edit the text.

- Change the title from **rptPlot5** to **Customer Sheet for Plot 5**.

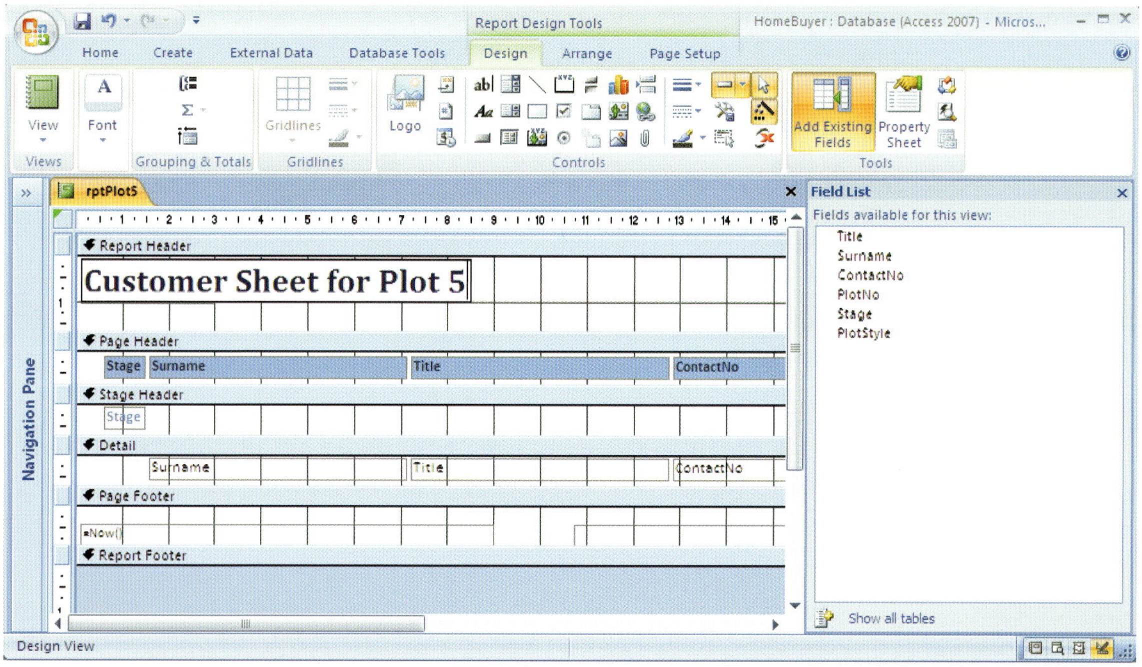

Figure 7.8

Click the **Print Preview** icon (**Report Design Tools**, **Design tab**, **Tools** group) and check that the report looks the way you want.

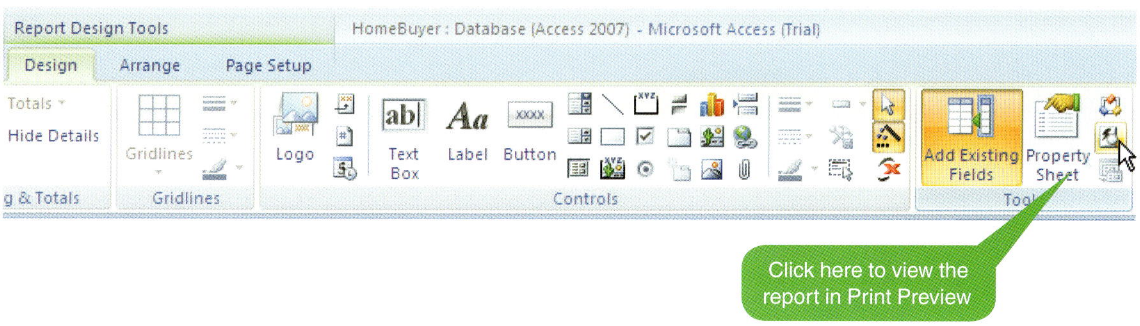

Figure 7.9

Adding fields to the report

It would be useful, when the list of customers interested in Plot 5 gets longer, to have a **Total** field which counts the number of customers interested in Plot 5.

Make sure the report is in **Design View** and since we are making a new field, that is one which does not occur in the **Field List** pane, make some more space to display the report by closing the pane (click the cross; see Figure 7.10).

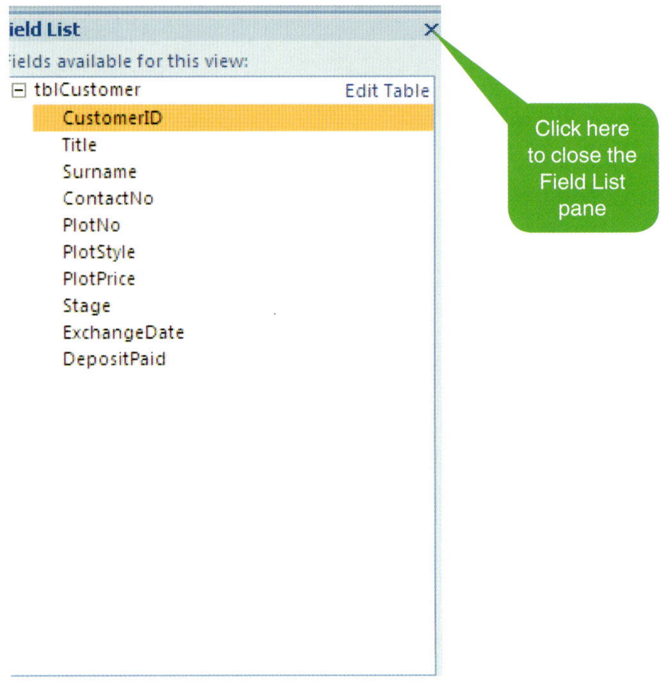

Figure 7.10

We want to put the total in the **Report Footer** – don't worry that there's no white page there yet. It will appear automatically when you place a field there.

- Click the **Text Box** button in the **Controls** group (see Figure 7.11).

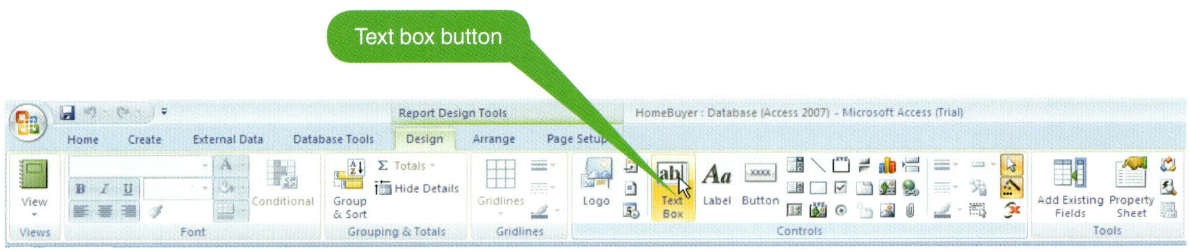

Figure 7.11

- Click below the report footer and drag to make a rectangular field.

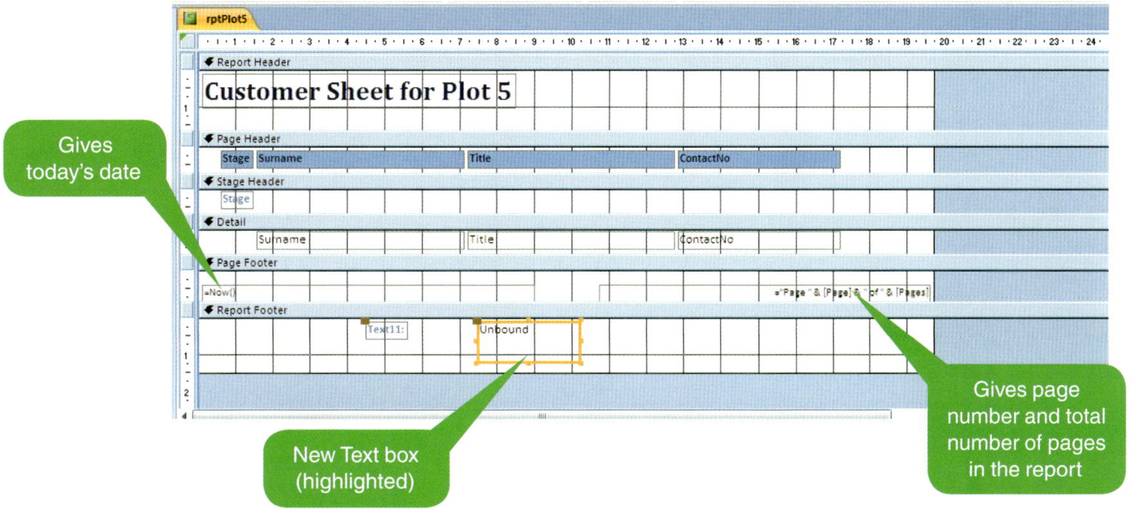

Figure 7.12

Make sure that the new text box is highlighted (it turns orange when highlighted; see Figure 7.12) and then click the **Properties** button (**Report Design Tools**, **Design** tab, **Tools** group).

The Properties give us the option of changing not only the appearance of the text box, but also how it functions. Each database object has its own list of associated properties which gives you considerable control of the design of a database.

In the **Properties** box, the text box will have a **Name** property something like **Text11** (the number may be different in your database).

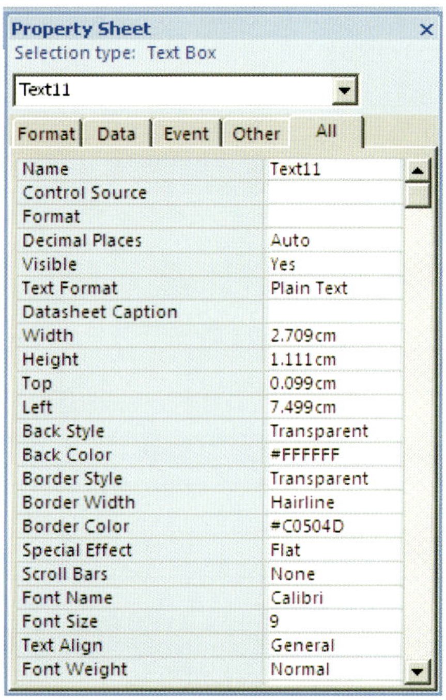

Figure 7.13

Change the name of the text box to **Total**.

In the **Control Source** property enter **=Count(*)**. This counts the number of records in the report, which equals the number of customers interested in Plot 5.

Click on the **Text14** label, then click again to edit the text. Change it to say **Total**.

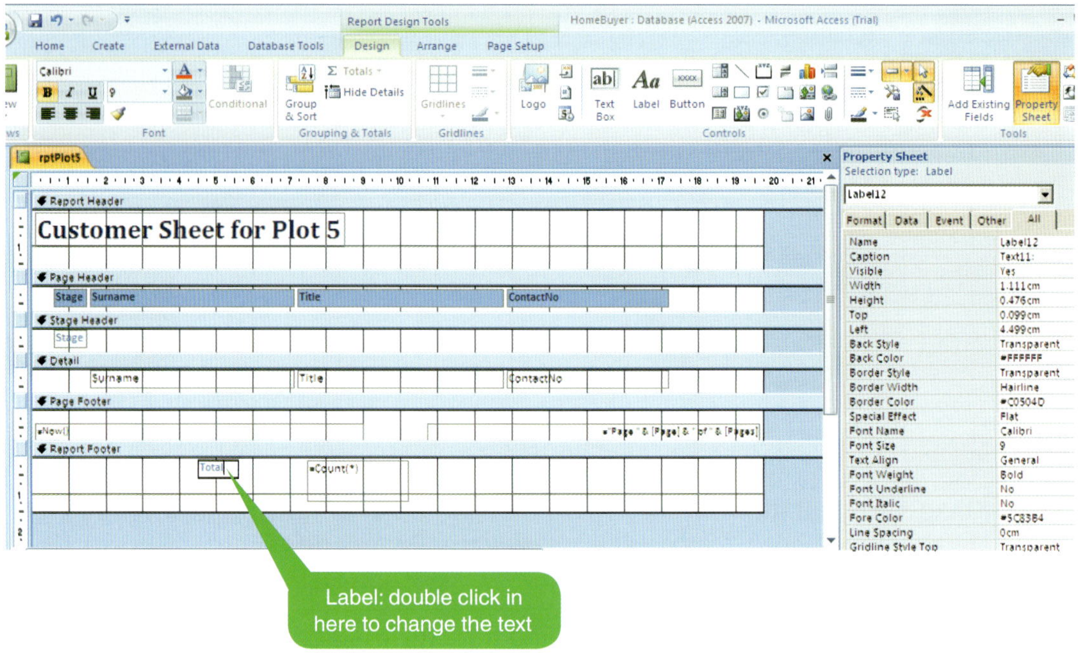

Figure 7.14

The **Total** field isn't quite where we want it.

Close the **Properties** pane to give a fuller view of the report.

Click and drag the **Total** field (careful to click on the **field**, not just the **label**) to the right edge of the report.

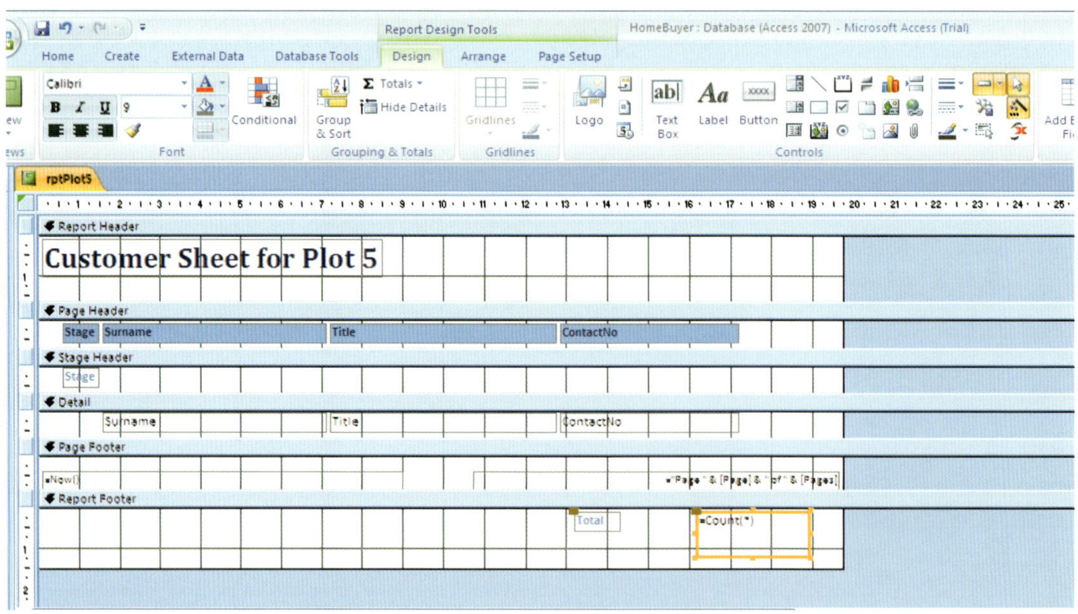

Figure 7.15

Return to **Print Preview** to check the results.

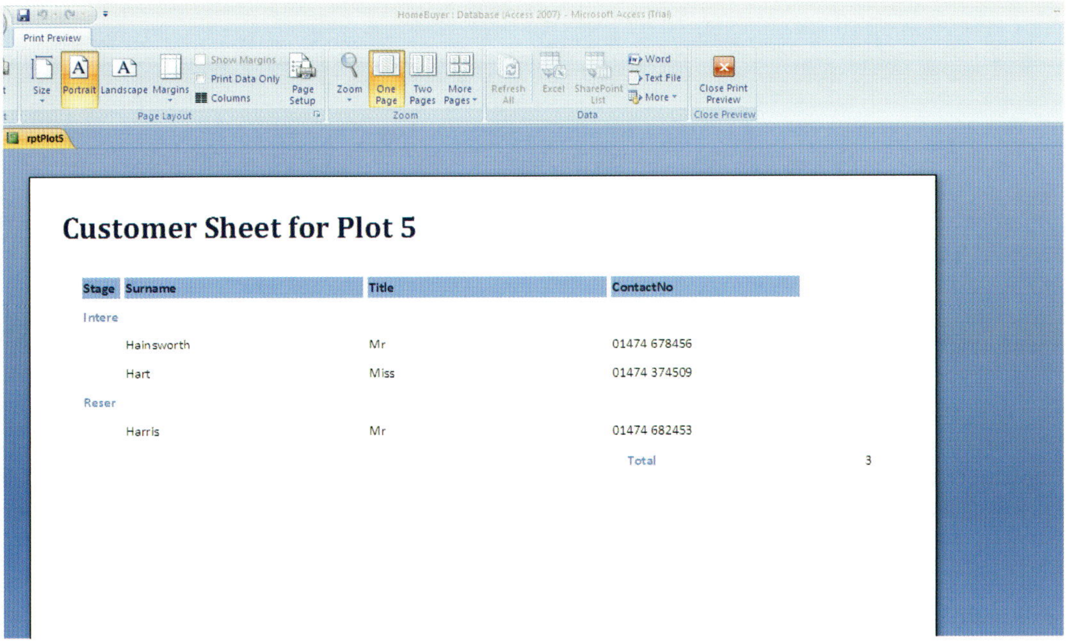

Figure 7.16

If you would like to do more to tidy up the appearance of the report, you can return to **Design View** and change fonts, add lines, etc. by opening the **Properties** for each object and experiment by changing the entries. The entries in the **Format** tab of the Properties are a good (and non-destructive!) place to start, but it is a good idea to do a '**Save**' before you begin. Remember that the **Undo** button on the **Quick Access Toolbar** is a convenient way of undoing unsuccessful experimental results.

Printing your report

- In **Print Preview** view click the **Print** button.
- Save and close your report (click the **Save** button on the **Quick Access Toolbar**; see Figure 7.17).

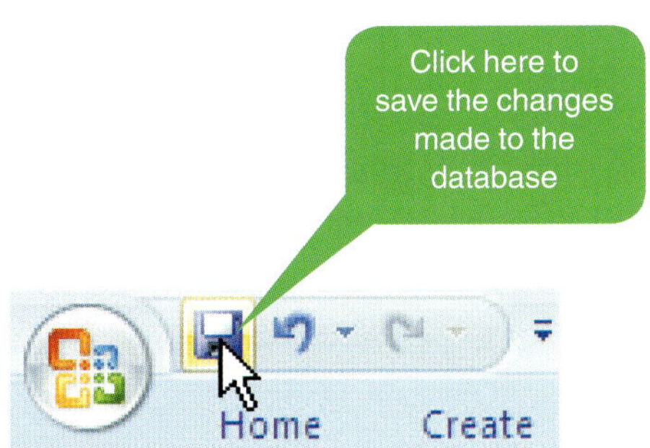

Figure 7.16

- Close the database and exit Access.

Tip:
You can switch between views of your database objects by using the View button on the Design tab.

Chapter 8 – Relational Database Design

Introduction

A **relational database** is one which contains two or more tables or **relations** linked by common fields. (A **relation** is just a jargon word for the links between **tables**.)

We will now look at creating a database with more than one table for the sales staff at Bentwells. This means we can make the database store more information and perform more useful functions. By doing this, we will be creating a relational database. Before creating this database it is important to understand some of the database theory.

A simple database like the **HomeBuyer** database consists of just one table of data. Each row in the table holds one record and each record has a primary key which uniquely identifies that record. This is known as a **flat file** database. We will now look at the difference between a flat file database and a relational database.

Problems with a flat file database

It is a common problem with many flat file databases that the same data is duplicated several times. To explain why, we will look at the example of the HomeBuyer database you have created.

Each plot has a different price depending on the style of house standing on it, and this information needs to be stored in the database. At the moment we have a column in the **Customer** table to store the price. However if there were 20 people interested in one plot, the price of that plot would have to be entered in the database 20 different times.

Also, it is likely that each customer may be interested in more than one plot. **Mr Hainsworth** might be interested in plots 1, 2 and 5. This means that there will have to be three records in the table for him and we will have to enter all his personal details (title, surname, contact number, etc.) in all three records.

The table would then look like the one in Table 8.1.

Title	Surname	ContactNo	PlotNo	PlotStyle	PlotPrice	Stage	ExchangeDate	DepositPaid
Mr	Hainsworth	01474 678456	1	Kenning	£165000	Interested		N
Mr	Hainsworth	01474 678456	2	Winnel	£145000	Interested		N
Mr	Hainsworth	01474 678456	5	Harrington	£185000	Interested		N
Mr	Hodson	01474 212394	1	Kenning	£165000	Interested		N
Mr	Stevenson	01474 665498	3	Scott	£210000	Reserved	1/12/2002	Y
Miss	Hart	01474 374509	5	Harrington	£185000	Interested		N
Mr	Ellis	01474 151884	2	Winnel	£145000	Exchanged	15/08/2002	Y
Mrs	Harris	01474 908635	4	Hamilton	£250000	Reserved	3/12/2002	N

Table 8.1

This table has several problems. For one thing the personal data for Mr Hainsworth (title, surname, etc.) has to be typed in three times, which is a waste of time. Second, it would be easy to make a spelling mistake in the surname in one of the records.

Title	Surname	ContactNo	PlotNo	PlotStyle	PlotPrice	Stage	ExchangeDate	DepositPaid
Mr	Hansworth	01474 678456	1	Kenning	£165000	Interested		N

Table 8.2

Now if you wanted to look up all the records for Mr Hainsworth only two records would be found and Mr Hainsworth would miss out on Plot 1!

Third, if Mr Hainsworth changed his telephone number (contact number) you would have to remember to change it in three different records, not just one.

A relational database

The solution to these problems is to hold the data in separate tables. We need a table for the customers and a different table for the plots. The two tables will need to be linked. A database that contains two or more linked tables is called a relational database. Before you learn how to design this sort of database you need to learn some new vocabulary.

Entity

An **entity** is a person or thing about which data is held. In our example there are two entities, **Customer** and **Plot**.

Attribute

An **attribute** is a piece of information about the entity. For example the attributes belonging to the entity **Customer** are **title, surname** and **contact no.**

? What attributes belong to the entity **Plot**? (Refer to Table 8.1.)

✓ **Plot number**, **Plot price** and **Plot style**.

Relationships

There are three different types of **relationship** between entities.

- **One-to-one**, e.g. husband and wife. A husband can have **one** wife and a wife can have **one** husband.
- **One-to-many**, e.g. football team and player. A football team has **many** players, but a player belongs to only **one** team.
- **Many-to-many**, e.g. student and subject. A student studies **many** subjects and a subject is studied by **many** students.

? Which of these relationships applies to Customer and Plot in the example above?

✓ Many-to-many: One customer can be interested in many plots, and one plot may have many customers interested in it.

Entity-relationship diagrams

Each of these relationships can be shown in an **Entity-Relationship (E-R)** diagram, as in Figure 8.1.

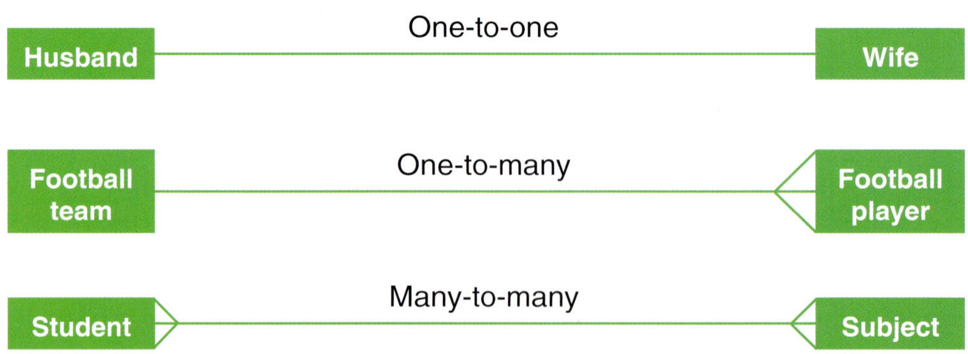

Figure 8.1: Entity-relationship diagrams.

Designing the database

Each entity needs its own table containing its own attributes. In addition each record in a table must have a field which uniquely identifies that record, the **primary key**, just as in the **HomeBuyer** database.

We will continue to use **CustomerID** as the key field for the **Customer** table. Each plot will have a unique number from 1 to 30, so we can use **PlotNo** as the key field for the **Plot** table.

Now the two tables look like this:

CustomerID	Title	Surname	ContactNo
201	Mr	Hainsworth	01474 678456
202	Mr	Hodson	01474 212394
203	Mr	Stevenson	01474 665498
204	Miss	Hart	01474 374509
205	Mr	Ellis	01474 151884
206	Mrs	Harris	01474 908635

Table 8.3: ***Customer*** *table.*

PlotNo	Style	Price
1	Kenning	£165,000
2	Winnel	£145,000
3	Scott	£210,000
4	Hamilton	£250,000
5	Harrington	£185,000
6	Harrington	£185,000
7	Scott	£210,000

Table 8.4: ***Plot*** *table.*

Note:
The customers have been given codes starting from 201 so they can be distinguished from plot numbers.

Linking the two tables

Hang on a minute! This is very neat but now we don't know who's interested in which plot.

Whenever there is a many-to-many relationship, a third table is required to link the two tables.

For this database, the link table will contain information specifying who is interested in which plot, and each record will contain **CustomerID** and **PlotNo**. This table will look like Table 8.5:

Tip:
The extra table will always contain the key fields from each of the original two tables. The two fields form a composite key in the third table.

CustomerID	PlotNo
201	1
201	2
201	5
202	1
203	3

Table 8.5

? Using Table 8.5 and the **Customer** and **Plot** Tables 8.3 and 8.4, can you list who is interested in which plot?

There is still some information missing, such as **stage, exchange date** and **deposit paid**. All this information is specific to both customer and plot, so belongs in the extra table alongside **CustomerID** and **PlotNo**. This extra table now looks like Table 8.6.

CustomerID	PlotNo	Stage	Exchange	DepositPaid
201	1	Interested		N
201	2	Interested		N
201	5	Reserved	1/12/02	Y
202	1	Reserved	2/12/02	Y
203	3	Exchanged	5/9/02	Y

Table 8.6: **CustomerPlot** *table*

Sometimes, a single field is not enough to uniquely identify a record. In Table 8.5 you would have to look at both **CustomerID** and **PlotNo** to know which record you were in, so both fields form part of the primary key. A primary key which consists of more than one field is sometimes called a **composite** key or **compound** key.

The three tables are now linked like this:

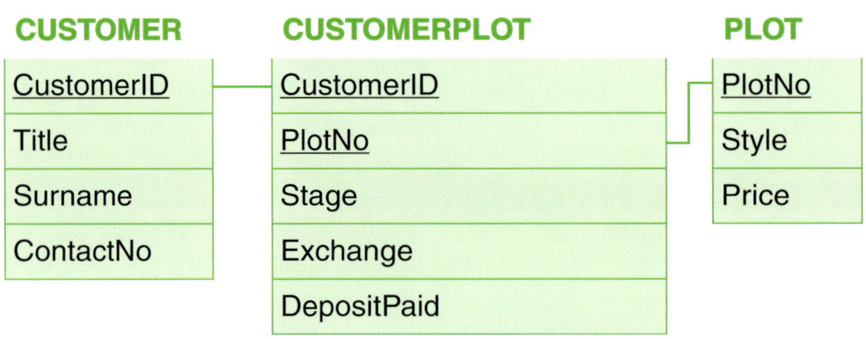

A fourth table?

Now we could easily design the database as described above – but there is still something that is not quite right. There is still some information that is needlessly being entered many times. Look at Table 8.4 and think what it is.

✓ It's the plot price. Since price depends on the style of house and not on the particular plot, ideally we should enter the price of each style of house into the database just once.

To do this, we need another table. This table will contain both **Style** and **Price**, and will look like this:

Tip:
Every attribute in a table should depend on the key, the whole key and nothing but the key! In this scenario the price depends only on the house style.

Style	Price
Kenning	£165,000
Winnel	£145,000
Scott	£210,000
Hamilton	£250,000
Harrington	£185,000

Table 8.7: ***HouseStyle*** *table*

What is the relationship between the entities **HouseStyle** and **Plot**? Consider:

- Each plot will have one house style
- Each house style might be used on many plots

The relationship between style and plot is therefore one-to-many:

Figure 8.2

We will call this new table the **HouseStyle** table. The key field in this table will be **Style**. If you wanted, you could add more fields to this table that are specific to a particular house style, such as number of bedrooms, size of garage, and whether or not it has an en-suite. For now we will keep it simple by just entering price.

Now we have four tables in the database, linked as shown in Figure 8.3.

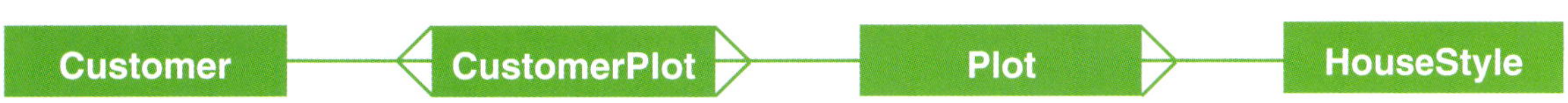

Figure 8.3

Chapter 9 – Creating Tables

New HomeBuyer database

We are going to create a new database as described in the previous chapter. It would be possible to modify the existing **HomeBuyer** database to be a relational database, but this is not recommended. Changing the database structure after data has been entered into the database can cause many problems in Access, and may result in data loss. Trying to fix these problems will take longer and be more complicated than just building a new database. We will call the new database the **AdvancedHomebuyer** database.

It is important to plan the structure of the database completely before implementing it. In the last chapter we decided which tables were needed and which fields were in each table. The next step is to specify which **data type** each field will be, just as we did for the original **HomeBuyer** database. In addition to the data type, in this database we will also specify the **field length** and **field type**.

We already know what information to hold about each entity. You can show the tables like this:

Tip:
Notice that the key fields in each table are underlined.

CUSTOMER (<u>CustomerID</u>, Title, Surname, ContactNo)

PLOT (<u>PlotNo</u>, Style)

CUSTOMERPLOT (<u>CustomerID</u>, <u>PlotNo</u>, Stage, Exchange, Deposit-Paid)

HOUSESTYLE (<u>Style</u>, Price)

Notice that in the **CustomerPlot** table the primary key is a **composite key** consisting of two fields. This is because a particular record cannot be identified without knowing both fields. For example, if a customer is interested in many plots, there will be several entries in this table for that customer. If many customers are interested in the same plot, there will be several records with the same **PlotNo**.

Naming conventions

The entity names in the database are Customer, Plot, CustomerPlot and HouseStyle. Each entity will be the basis of a table. Recall that when naming tables you should put the letters tbl in front. The table names in the database will be tblCustomer, tblPlot, tblCustomerPlot and tblHouseStyle.

The field names in each table will be the same as the attribute names for each entity.

The tables are listed below along with all their attributes. These tables, along with the Entity-Relationship diagrams, are all you need to design the **structure** of your database.

Field name	Data type	Field length/type
CustomerID	Number	Long Integer
Title	Text	4
Surname	Text	20
ContactNo	Text	15

Table 9.1: tblCustomer.

Field name	Data type	Field length/type
PlotNo	Number	Long Integer
Style	Text	20

Table 9.2: tblPlot.

Field name	Data type	Field length/type
CustomerID	Number	Long Integer
PlotNo	Number	Long Integer
Stage	Text	10
Exchange	Date/Time	–
DepositPaid	Y/N	–

Table 9.3: tblCustomerPlot.

Field name	Data type	Field length/type
Style	Text	20
Price	Currency	–

Table 9.4: tblHouseStyle.

Tip: CustomerID and PlotNo in tblCustomerPlot must have the same data type and field size as the same records in tblCustomer and tblPlot because they have to be linked later.

Now we've finished designing the structure, it's time to load up Access.

Implementing the database

Open **Access**, then click **Blank Database** in the centre pane.

A window opens as shown in Figure 9.1, asking you to select a folder and a name for your new database.

Figure 9.1

- Use the **Browse** button to find the folder **BentwellsBuilders** and double click it.
- In the **File Name** box, type the name **AdvancedHomebuyer** (no spaces), and click the **OK** button.

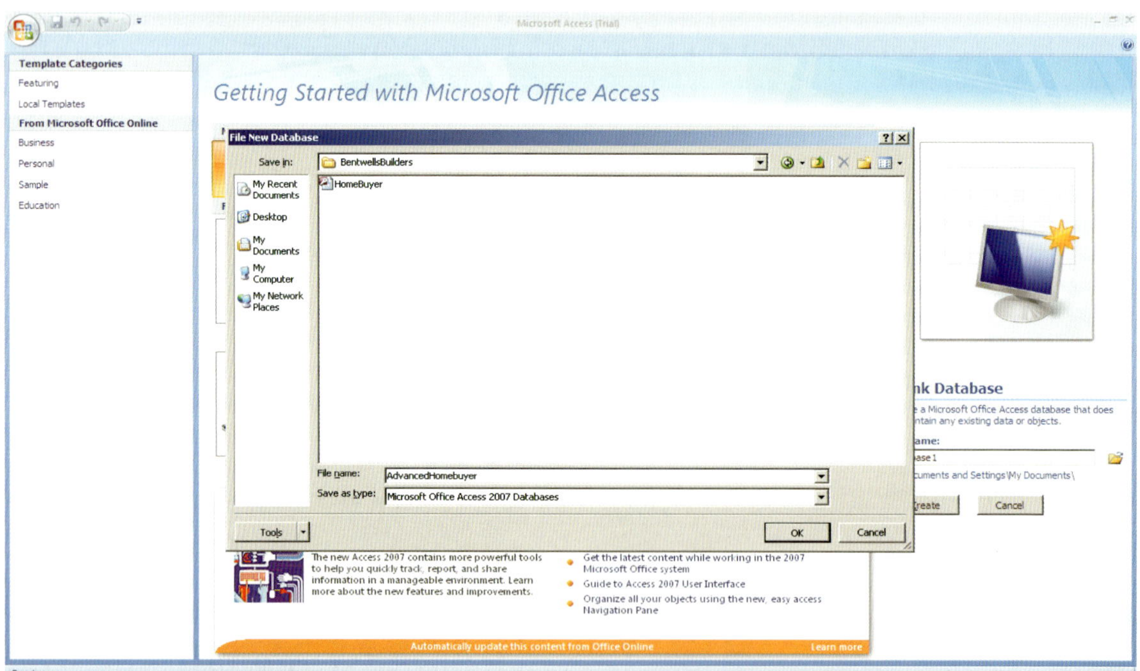

Figure 9.2

The **File New Database** dialogue box closes, in the **Blank Database** pane click the **Create** button; Access will automatically add the file extension **.accdb**.

Creating the tables

Swap to the **Create** tab and click the **Table** button; see Figure 9.3.

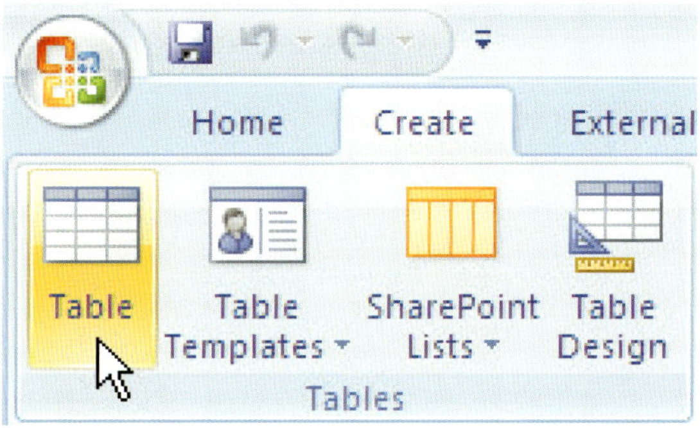

Figure 9.3

A new table opens in **Datasheet View**. Since we need to design the table before adding data, switch to **Design View** using the **View** button (just beneath the **Office** button).

Before displaying the table in design view you are asked to select a name for the new table and then to save it. Type in the name tblCustomer and then click **OK** to save; see Figure 9.4.

Figure 9.4

The **Table Design** window appears.

Look back at the structure of the **tblCustomer** table in Table 9.1. All these fields need to be entered in the new table.

Enter the first field name, **CustomerID**, and tab to the **Data Type** column.

Click the down-arrow and select the field type **Number**.

Tab to the **Description** column and type **This is the Key field**.

You will probably find that Access has already set this field as the primary key; if this is not the case, click in the row header and then click the **Primary Key** button.

Tip:
There are several different sorts of Number field. You can see them by clicking the down-arrow next to Long Integer under Field Properties. Leave this Number field as Long Integer.

Notice that the **Field Size** under **Field Properties** is already set to **Long Integer**.

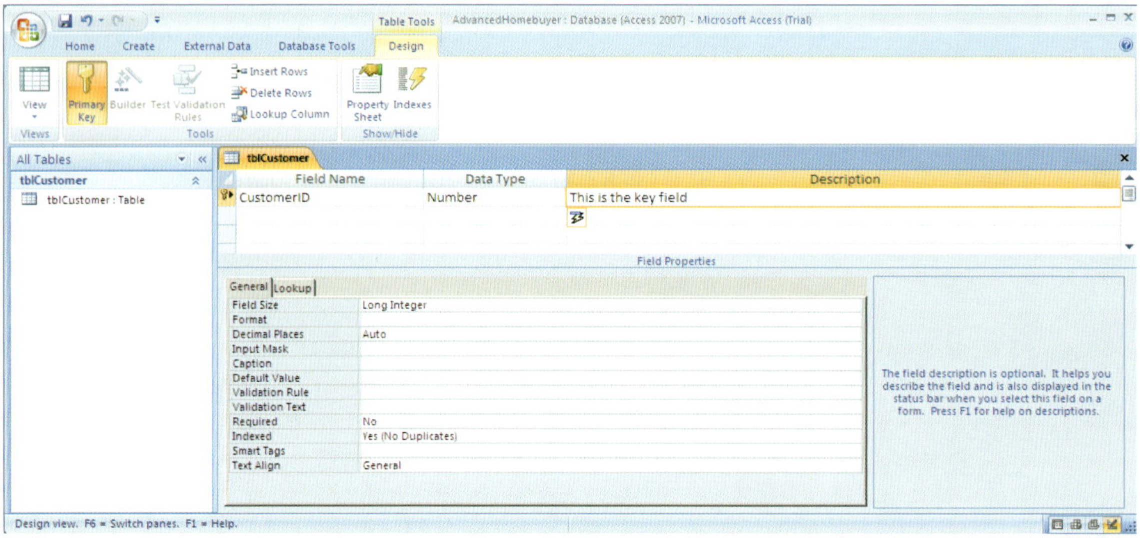

Figure 9.5

Entering other fields

Now you can enter all the other fields, referring to Table 9.1 for the field names, data types and field length/size.

Your table should now look like Figure 9.6.

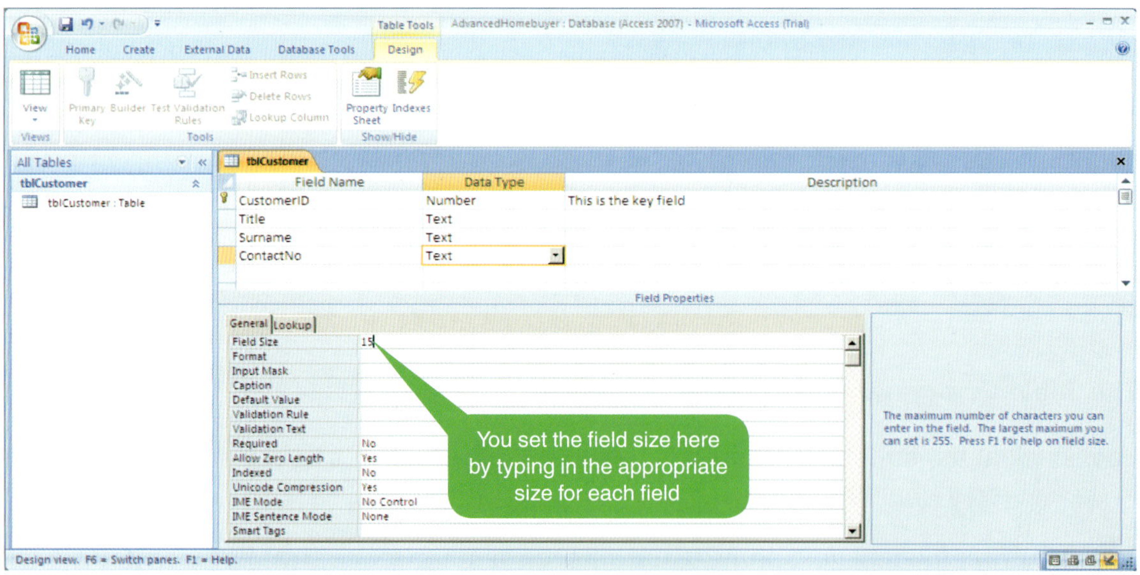

Figure 9.6

Close the table; you will be prompted to save the table:

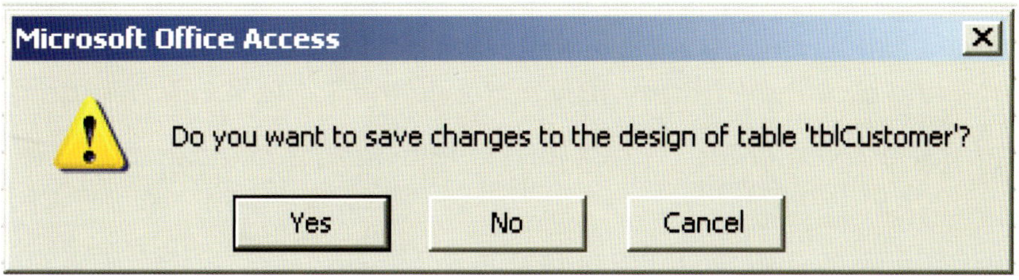

Figure 9.7

Click **Yes**.

Creating tblPlot

Switch to the **Create** tab and click the **Table** button. A new table is inserted in the database.

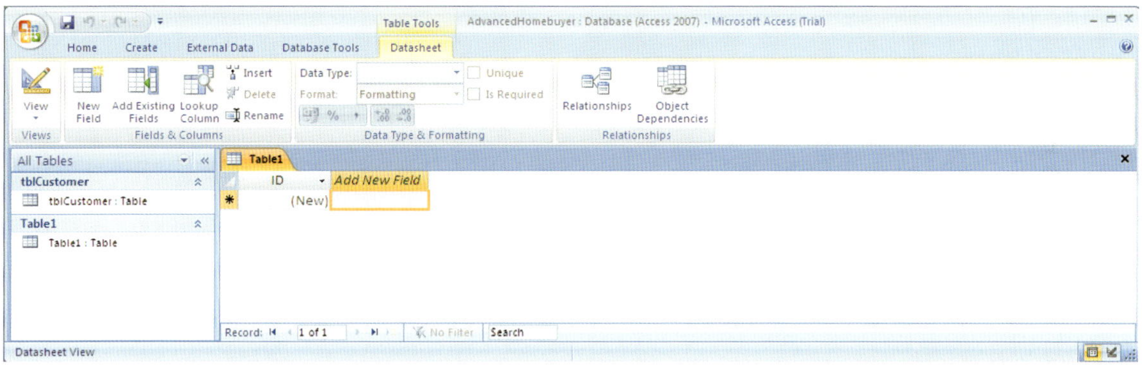

Figure 9.8

Switch to **Design View** (use the **View** button visible on the **Home** tab). You will be prompted to save the table – enter the table name tblPlot and click **OK**.

Using Table 9.2, enter each field in **tblPlot** along with its data type.

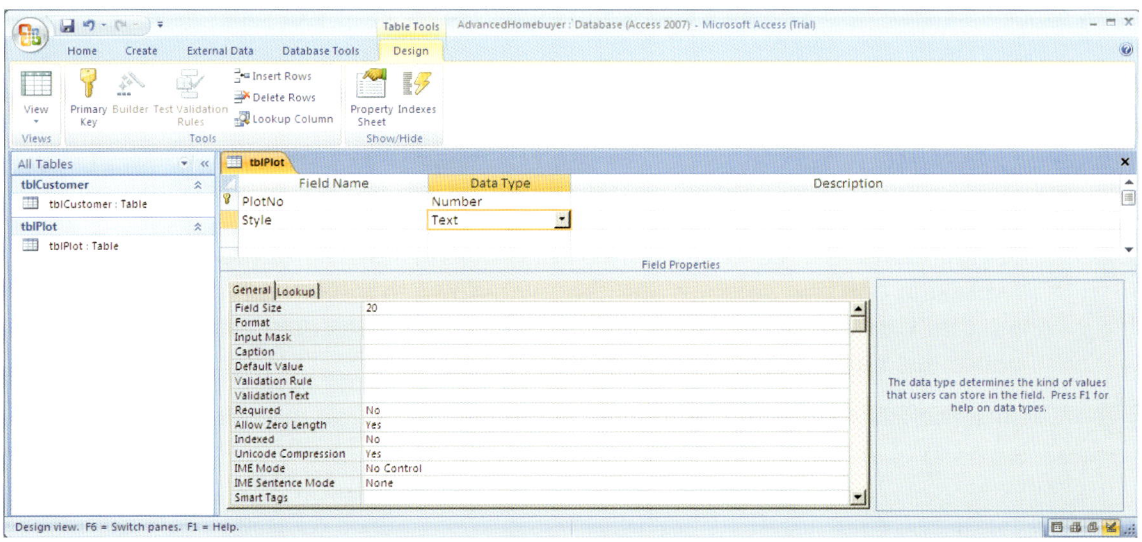

Figure 9.9

Tip:
If you have named the table wrongly, or made a spelling mistake, right click the table name in the Navigation pane and select Rename from the shortcut menu.

- When you have entered all the fields in **tblPlot** check that you have the field **PlotNo** as the primary key. If not, then click in the row header next to its field name and click the **Primary Key** button in the **Table Tools Design** tab.
- Remember to enter the correct field lengths and formats in the **Field Properties** (look at Table 9.2).
- Close the table and save the changes.

Creating tblHouseStyle

- Create **tblHouseStyle** in the same way, using Table 9.4. Remember to check and if necessary create the **Key field**.

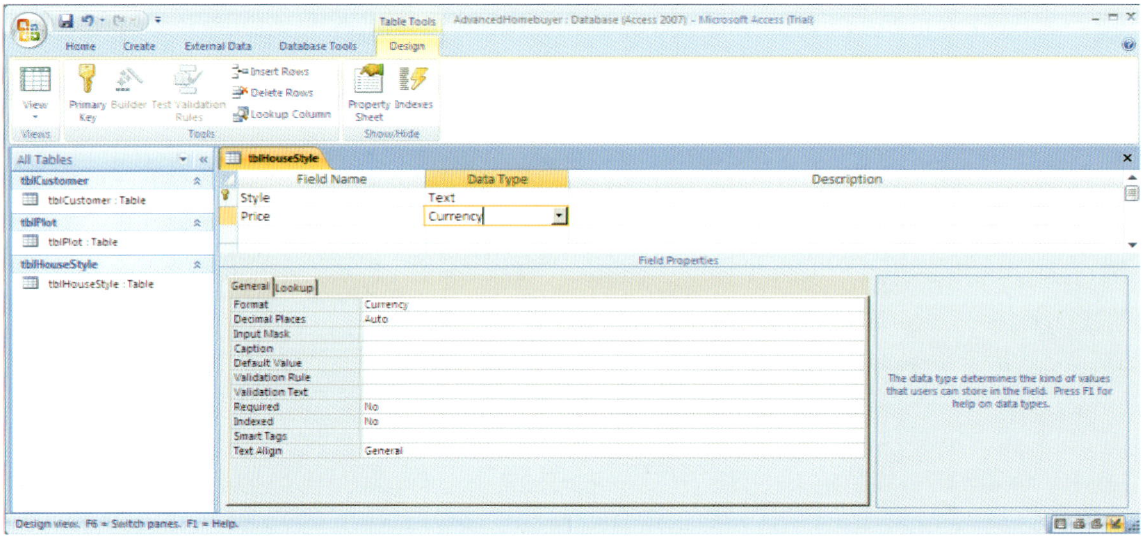

Figure 9.10

- Close the table and save the changes when prompted.

Tip:
The row selectors are the small boxes to the left of the Field Name box, which turn a darker blue when selected by clicking and orange when a field name or data type are selected.

Creating a composite key field

- Create a fourth new table for **tblCustomerPlot**.
- Enter the field names and types using Table 9.3.

This table has a primary key which consists of both fields. To define the primary key:

- Using the mouse, highlight the two fields **CustomerID** and **PlotNo** in the table, by clicking one row selector and dragging down to the other (you are likely to find that **CustomerID** has already been set by Access as a Primary Key but ignore this and just carry on).
- Click the **Primary Key** icon on the **Table Tools Design** tab (Figure 9.11).

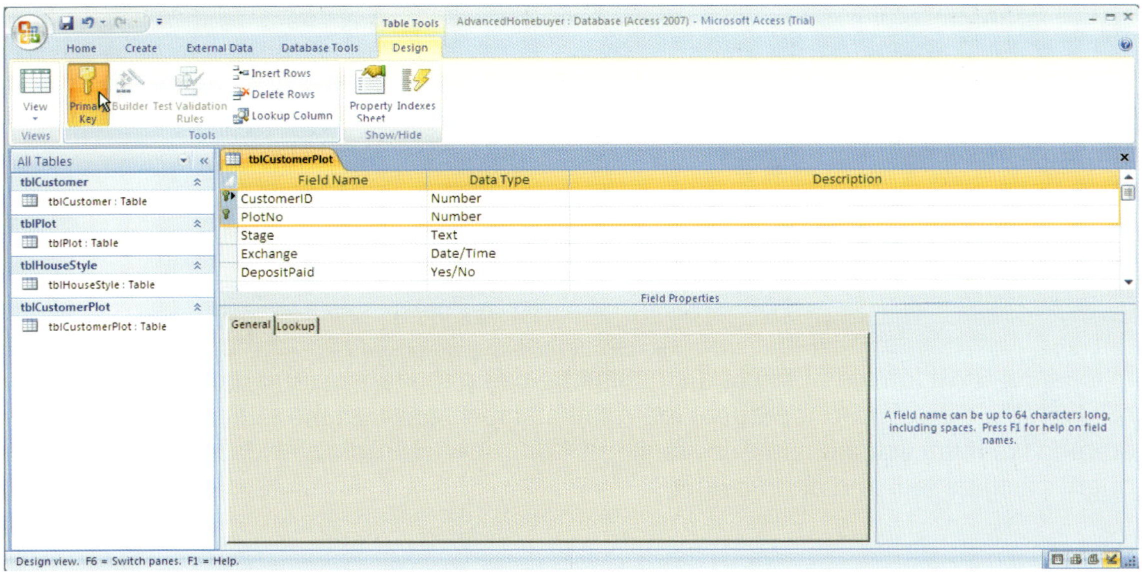

Figure 9.11

Default values

Most of the entries in the **Stage** field will be **Interested**. It would save time if this value automatically appeared when entering a new record in the **tblCustomerPlot** table.

- Click anywhere in the **Stage** field. Under **Field Properties**, enter **Interested** in the **Default Value** row.
- Close the table and database, saving changes when prompted.
- Exit Access.

Chapter 10 – Setting up Relationships

In Chapter 8 we looked at the relationships between the tables, and drew entity-relationship diagrams to represent the relationships. Now that the tables have been created we must link them in Access. If the **AdvancedHomebuyer** database is not open, navigate to it and open it now.

Relationships window

Switch to the **Database Tools** tab and click the **Relationships** button.

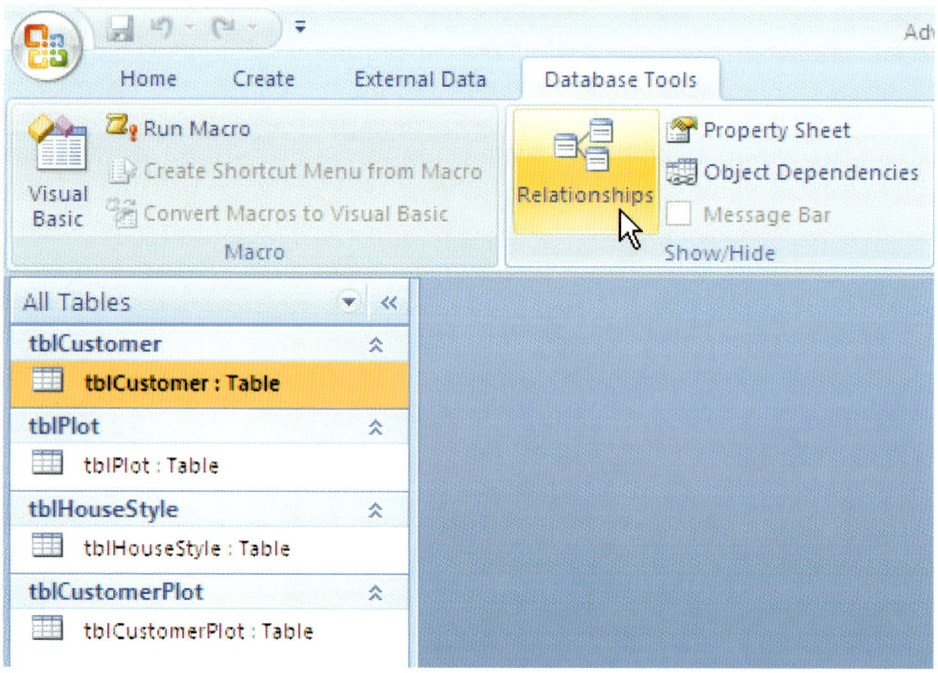

Figure 10.1

The **Show Table** window will appear:

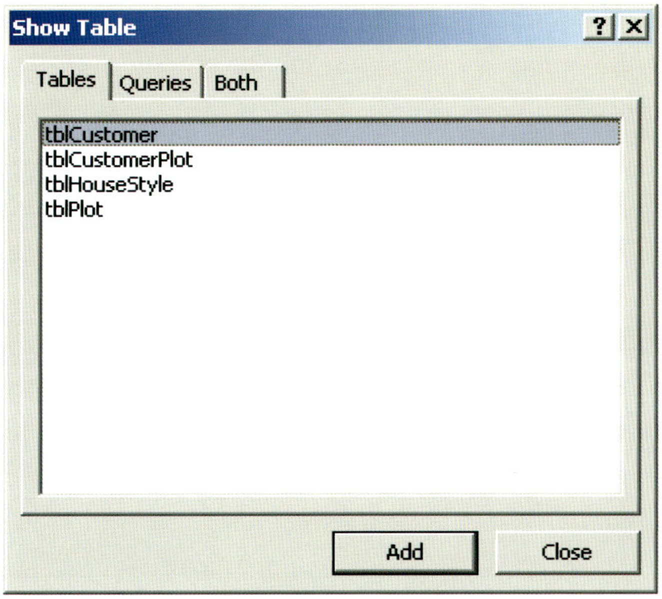

Figure 10.2

We want to form relationships between all four tables, so we will want all the tables to appear in the **Relationships** window.

- Highlight each one in turn and click **Add.**
- Click **Close.**

All four tables should now be in the **Relationships** window as shown in Figure 10.3:

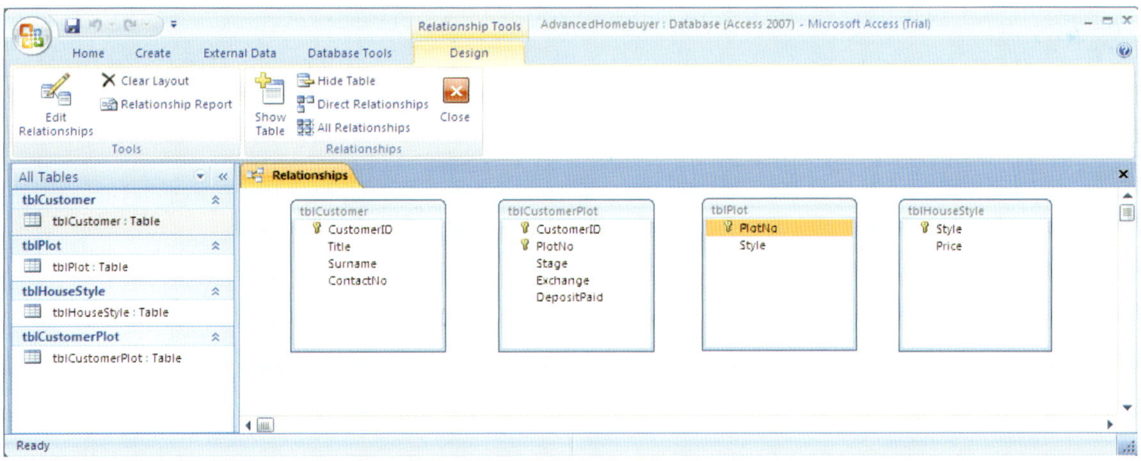

Figure 10.3

Tip:
You can highlight all of the tables by dragging over them and then add them all at once by clicking Add. It is useful to rearrange the tables as in Figure 10.3. You do this by clicking in the blue title bar of the table you wish to move and drag it to its new location.

Creating a relationship

Recall from Chapter 8 that we want a **one-to-many** relationship between **tblCustomer** and **tblCustomerPlot**.

- Click and drag the field **CustomerID** from **tblCustomer** and drop it onto the field **CustomerID** in **tblCustomerPlot**.

Tip:
Enforcing referential integrity means that you will not be allowed to add a record to tblCustomerPlot until you have added a record with the same CustomerID to tblCustomer.

The **Edit Relationships** window will appear:

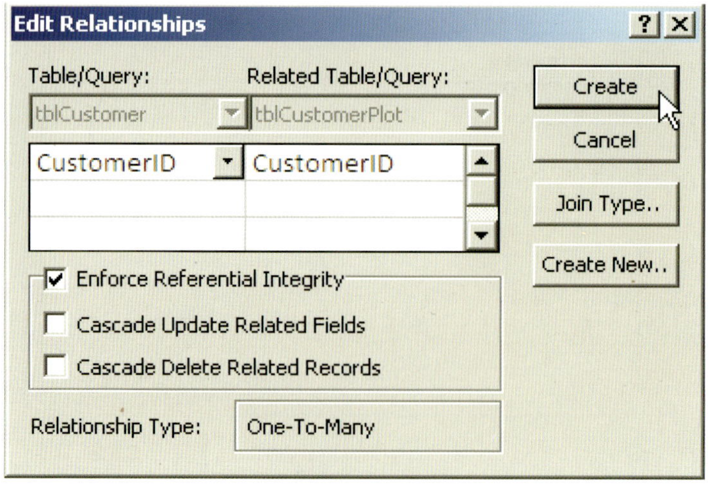

Figure 10.4

- Click the box marked **Enforce Referential Integrity** to select it, and then click **Create**.

You have now created a relationship between those two tables. Now you have to do the same for the other relationships:

- Click and drag the field **PlotNo** from **tblPlot** and drop it onto the field **PlotNo** in **tblCustomerPlot**.

Again, the **Edit Relationships** window appears.

- Click **Enforce Referential Integrity**, then click **Create**.
- Now create the one-to-many relationship between **tblHouseStyle** and **tblPlot**. Use the **Style** field to link the two tables, and this time don't check **Enforce Referential Integrity**.
- Rearrange the tables by clicking and dragging them, just to neaten it up a bit.

The **Relationships** window should now look like Figure 10.5.

Tip:
Don't worry if your window doesn't look like this – you can follow the instructions below to edit the relationships.

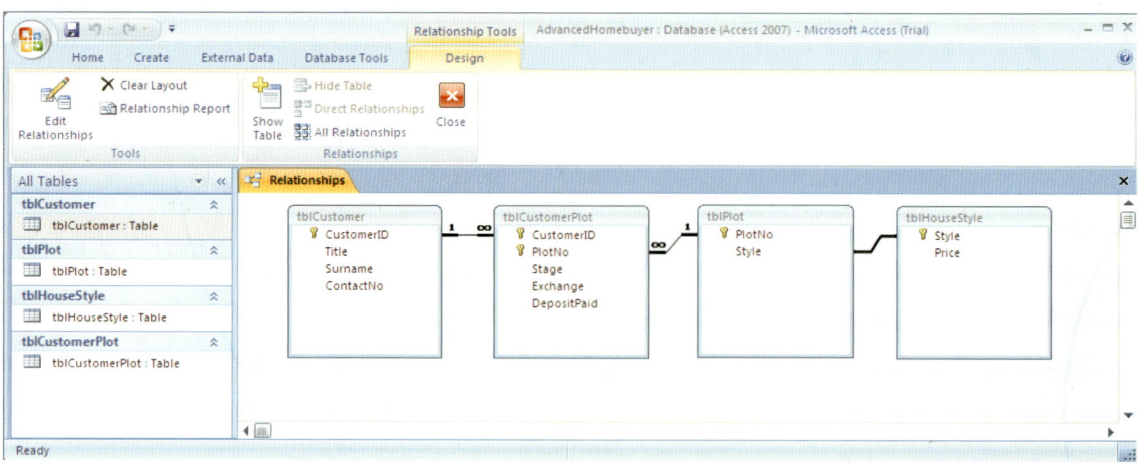

Figure 10.5

Editing relationships

It's easy to delete or edit a relationship:

- Right click on the relationship (represented by a line) between **tblPlot** and **tblHouseStyle**.

A shortcut menu appears as shown in Figure 10.6:

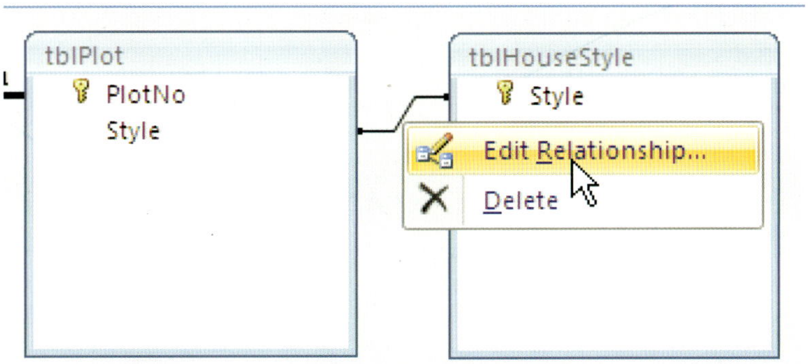

Figure 10.6

- Clicking the **Edit Relationship** option takes you to the **Edit Relationship** dialogue box shown in Figure 10.4; clicking the **Delete** key causes the following warning to appear:

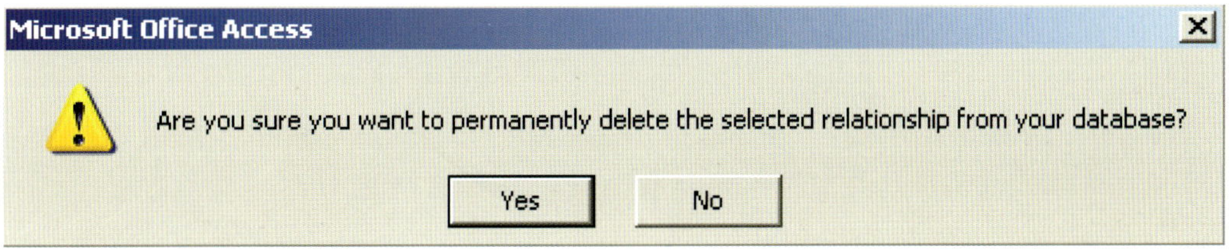

- If you click **Yes**, you will notice that the relationship has been deleted.

Now change the relationships back so they look like they did in Figure 10.5.

Word of warning

When there is no data in the database it is very easy to edit the relationships. Once you have entered data, it will still be possible to edit the relationships but this is not advisable. If you change a relationship after data has been entered, Access may get confused, and you could find obscure error messages appearing at inconvenient moments.

Saving the relationships

When you are satisfied that the relationships are correct, click the **Close** icon to return to the Database window. The relationships will automatically be saved, but you will be asked if you want to save the layout changes. Click **Yes**.

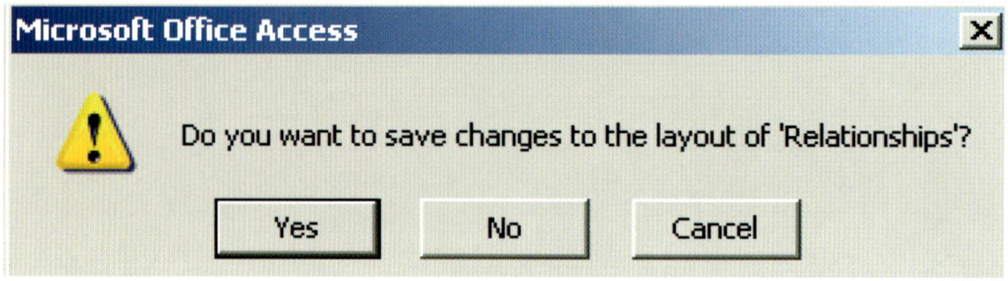

You can now re-save your database and exit Access, or continue to the next chapter.

Chapter 11 – Forms and Command Buttons

User interface

You need to consider how the users interact with your computer application – how they choose what to do next, how they enter data and so on. You need to create an attractive **user interface** so that it is easy to enter data and to navigate around the various options.

We will start by creating a form to allow the user to input data about plots. This form will be used to enter the plots as they are released by the builder for sale.

Creating a new form

- Load up the **AdvancedHomebuyer** database.

One of the options is to use a **wizard**. This is usually the quickest method, and the one you would normally use to create a simple form.

The only problem with wizards is that they do so much for you that it is sometimes difficult to see how to go back and change something. As a result people often start the whole form again if they have made a mistake in the form wizard – thus it can take longer than just learning how to create the form yourself.

For this reason we will not use a wizard this time, and you will see how easy it is to create the form yourself.

- In the Database window switch to the **Create** tab on the **Ribbon** and click the **Form Design** button.

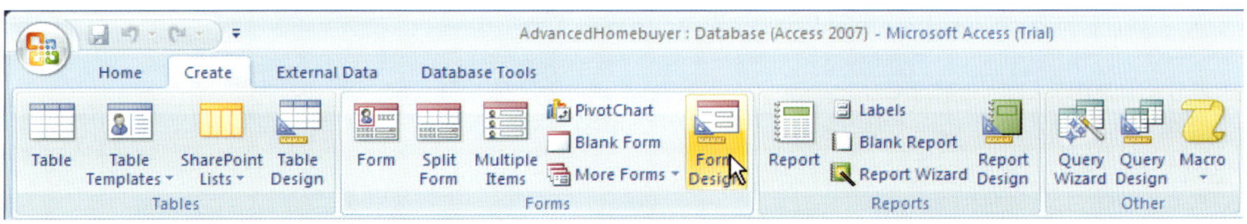

Figure 11.1

- A new form loads (the object with grid lines). Click the **Add Existing Fields** button.

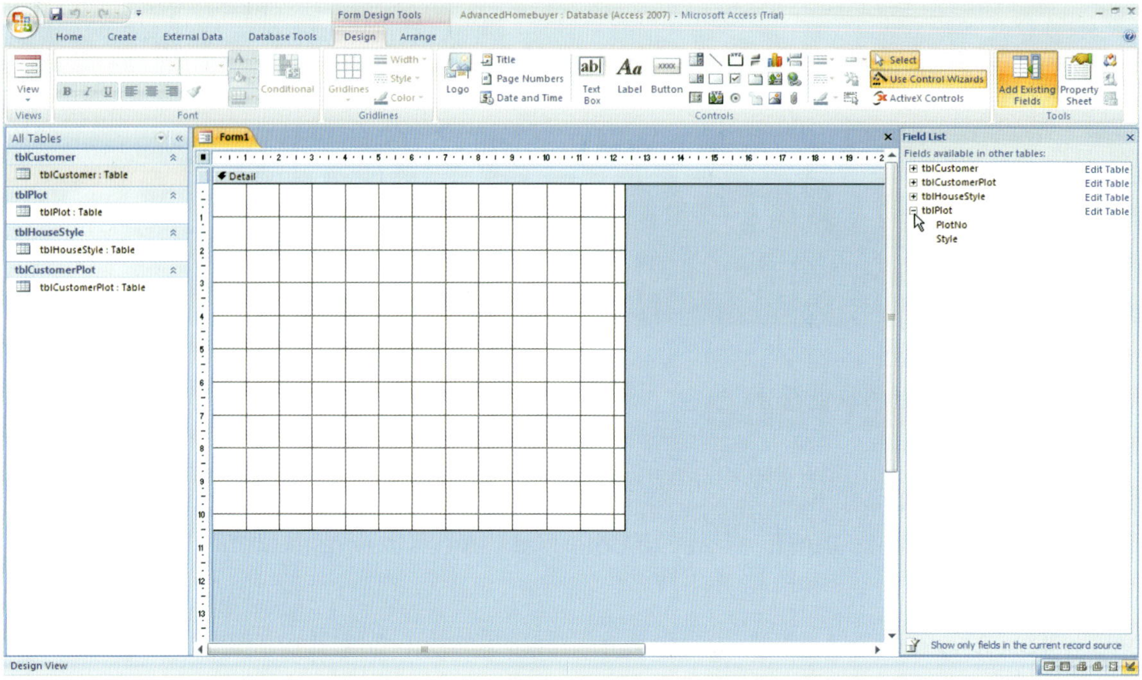

Figure 11.2

Find the reference to **tblPlot** in the **Field List** pane and click the small **+** symbol next to the table name to reveal the fields in the table; see Figure 11.2.

Click on **PlotNo** and drag it onto the form area. Do the same with **Style** and arrange the text boxes and their associated labels as shown in Figure 11.3.

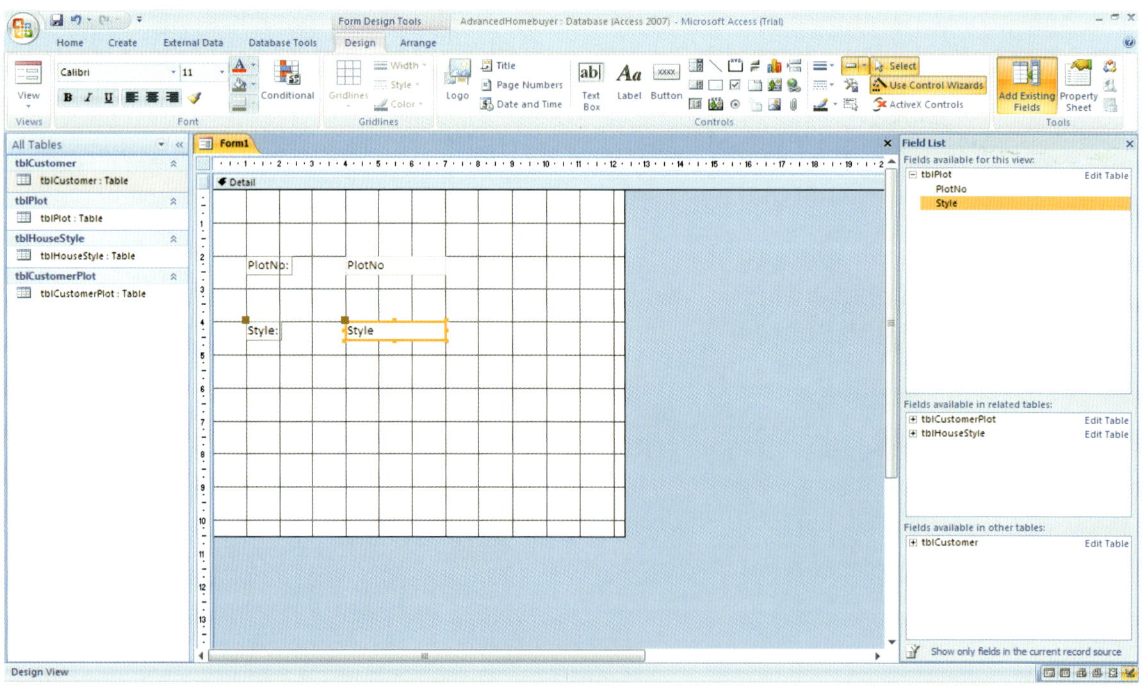

Figure 11.3

Change to Form View (Figure 11.4).

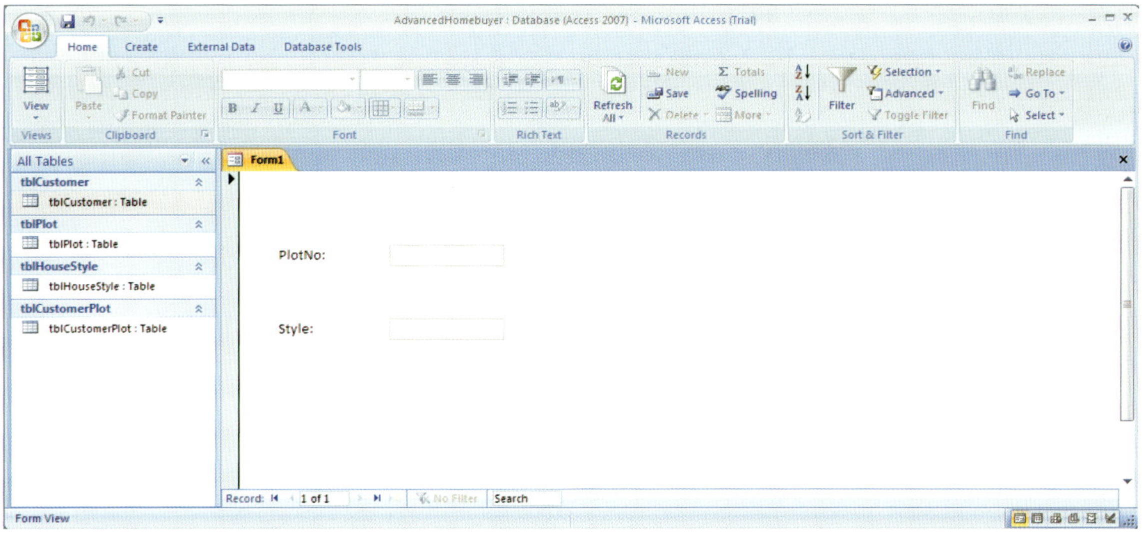

Figure 11.4

- Save the form by clicking the **Save** button on the **Quick Access Toolbar**.
- Type the name of the form **frmPlot** into the **Save As** dialogue box.

Figure 11.5

- Check that your form is saved by clicking the down-arrow in the **Navigation** pane and then selecting Forms. You should find your form listed as shown in Figure 11.6.

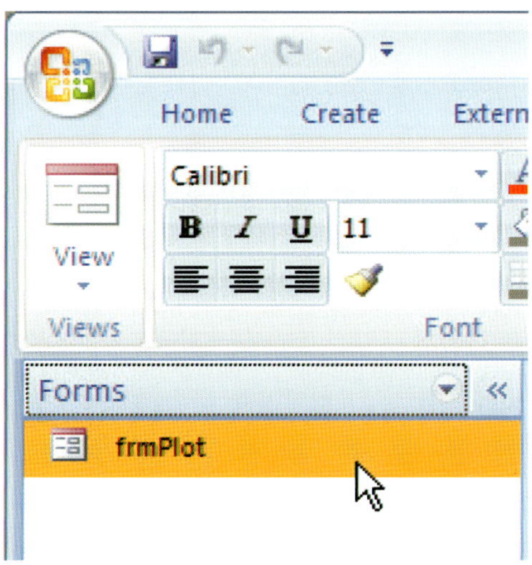

Figure 11.6

Added confirmation (and another method of navigation around the database) can be found in the central pane where both the table and form appear as names on the tabs.

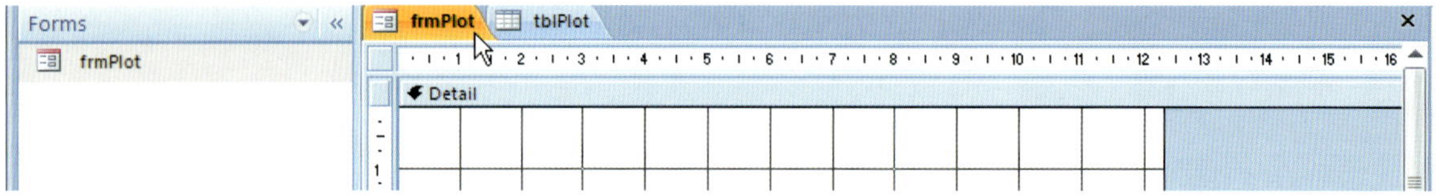

Figure 11.7

Form View

There are two views you can use to look at a form. **Design View** is the view you are in at the moment, and is used for editing the form. **Form View** is the view you would use if you were actually entering or just viewing the data.

Click the **Form View** icon.

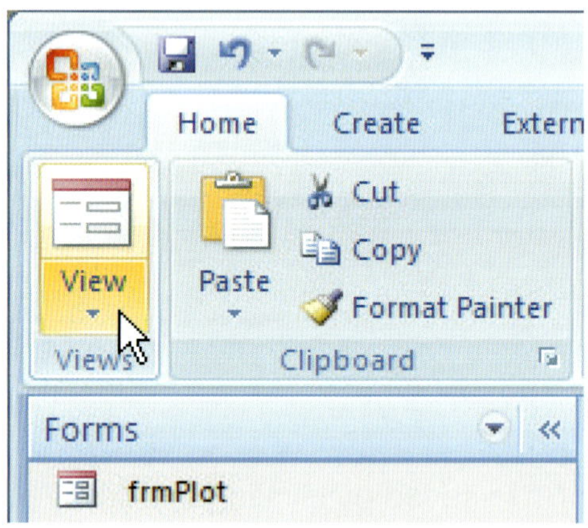

Figure 11.8

The form will now appear in **Form View**.

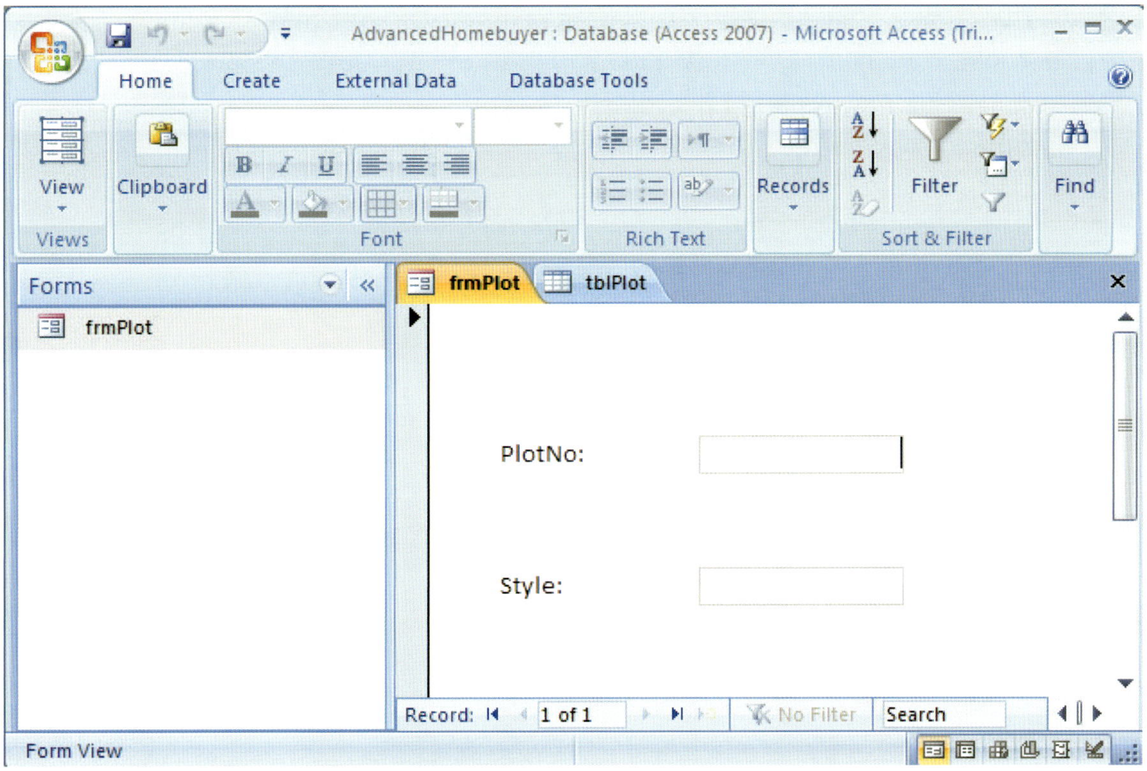

Figure 11.9

Modifying the form

There are two changes that can be made to the form to make data entry quicker and easier.

The first is to make one of the fields into a **list box**. We will make the **Style** field a **list box** so that you can pick **Style** from a list instead of typing it in.

List boxes

For this list box, we will design it so that it displays all the styles that are entered in the **tblHouseStyle** table. This means the list box will be empty until you enter something in that table.

- Return to **Design View** by clicking the **Design View** icon.
- Click the **List Box** icon in the **Controls** group.

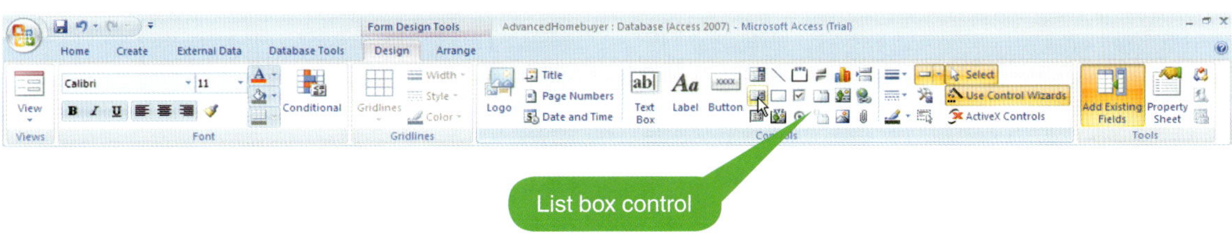

Figure 11.10

Click about a field's width to the right of the **Style** field, and drag out a rectangle. The List Box Wizard loads (patience – it may be a bit slow).

Select the option **I want the list box to look up the values in a table or query**. Click **Next**.

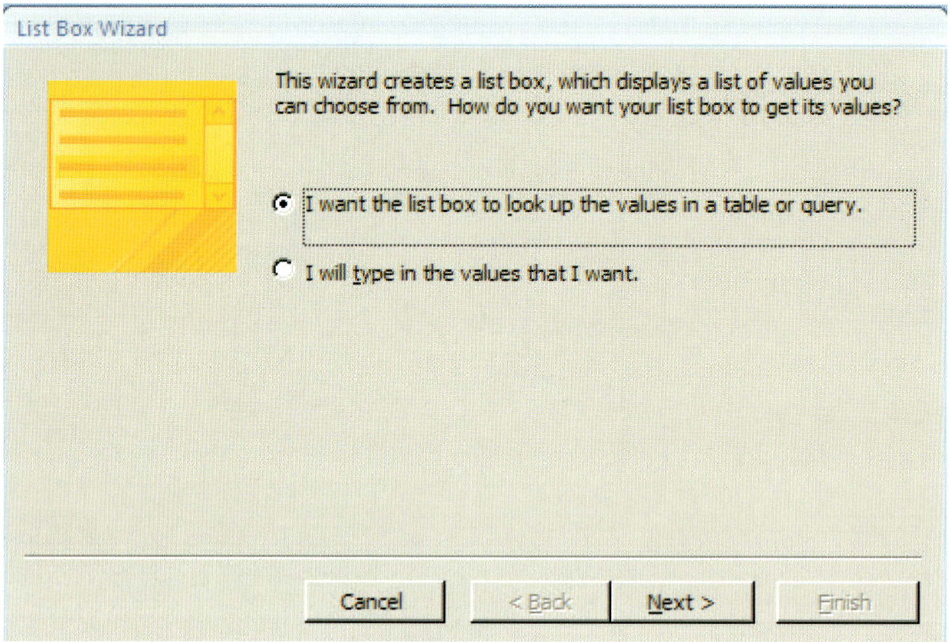

Figure 11.11

Select **tblHouseStyle** and click **Next**.

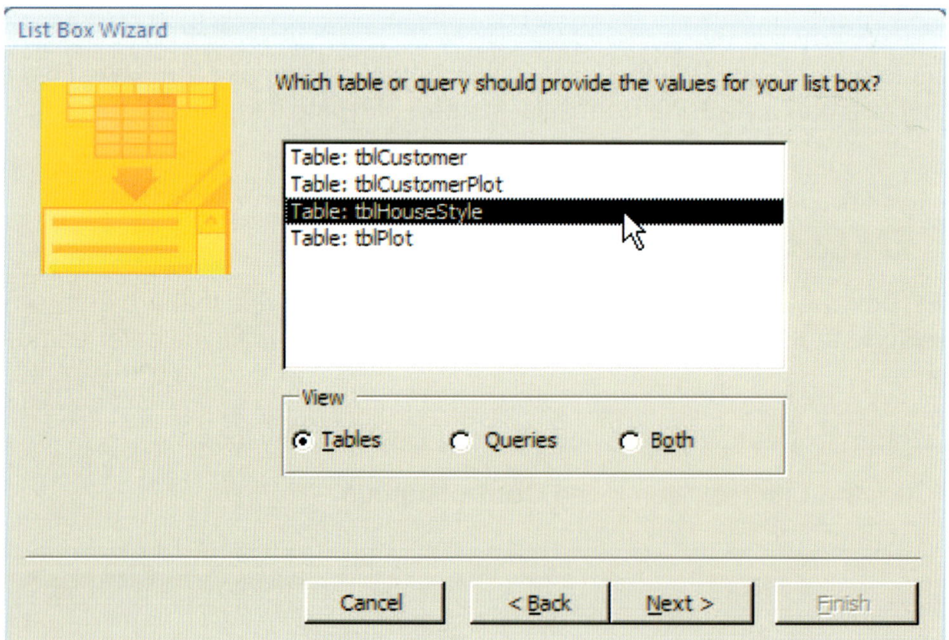

Figure 11.12

It might be nice to have the price appear alongside the style in the list box, so click >> so that both **Style** and **Price** appear in the right-hand window. Click **Next**.

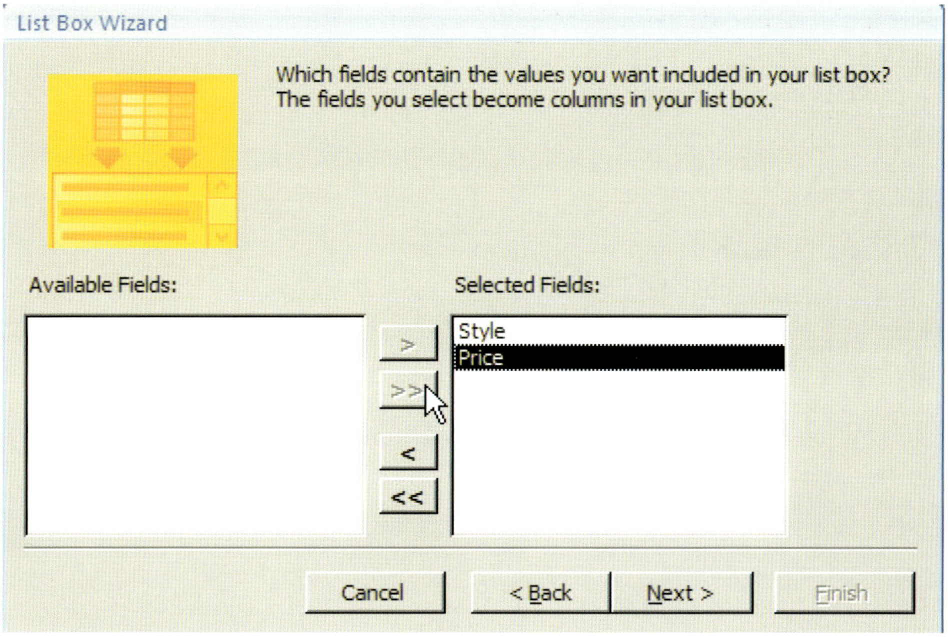

Figure 11.13

It would be useful to have the styles of houses sorted into alphabetical order so make the following changes in the next window of the wizard. Click **Next**.

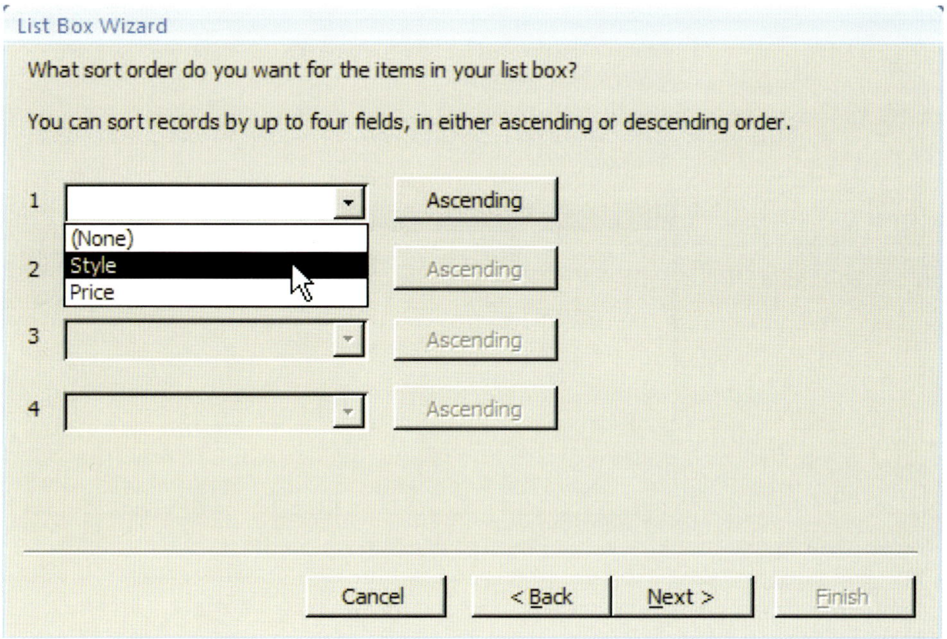

Figure 11.14

Remember that the **Style** field is used as a key field, so uncheck **Hide Key Column** to display both fields as in Figure 11.15. Click **Next**.

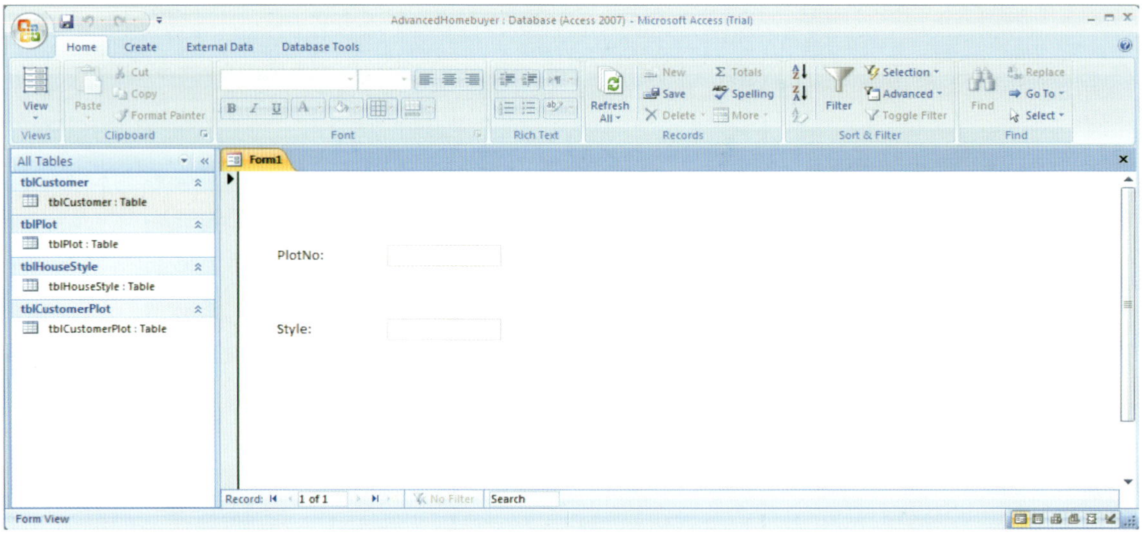

Figure 11.15

You want the database to store the **Style**, so make sure **Style** is highlighted. Click **Next**.

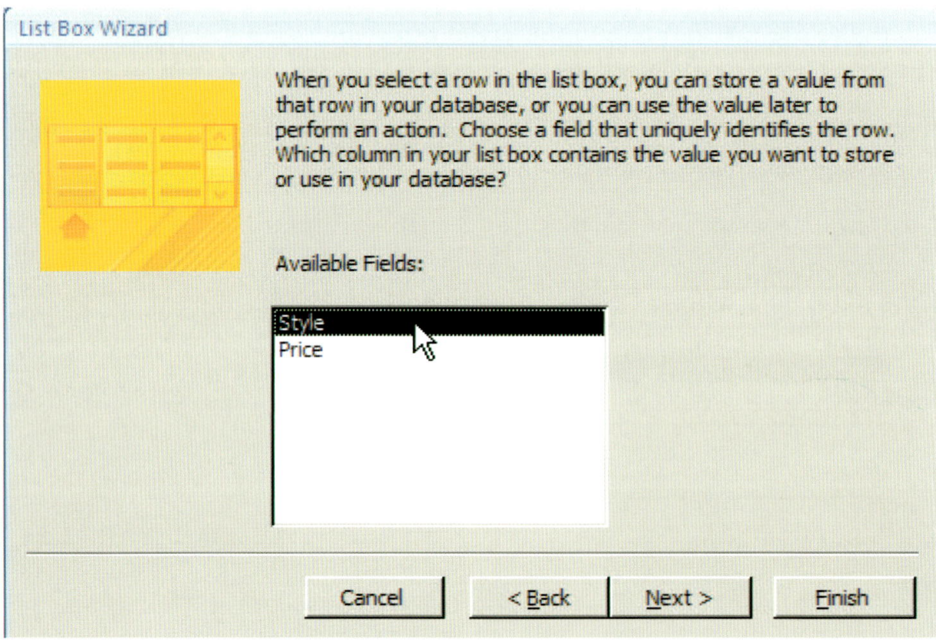

Figure 11.16

In this window, select **Style** from the list by **Store that value in this field**. Click **Next**.

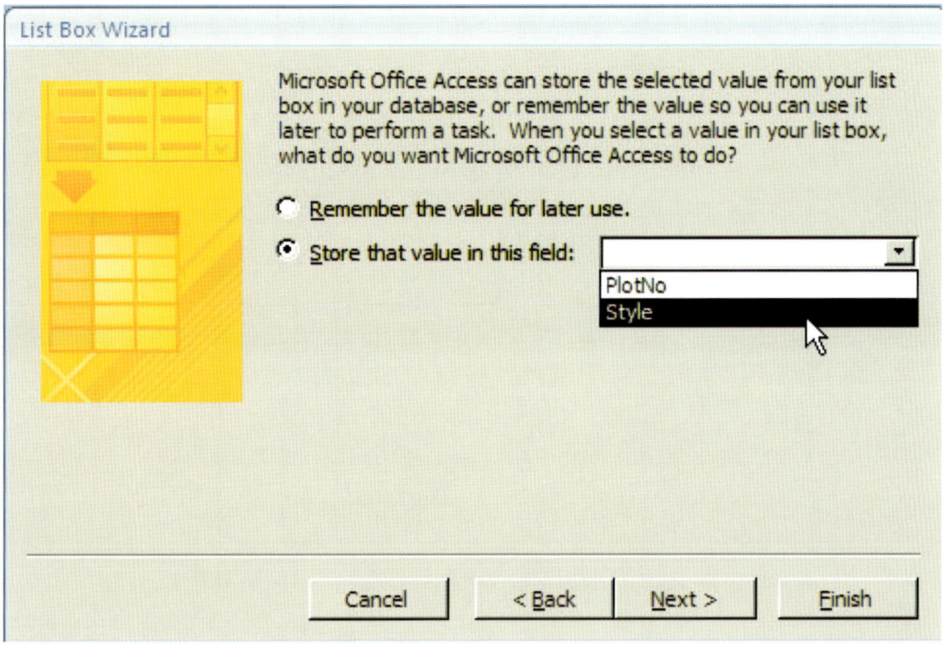

Figure 11.17

- Enter **Style** as the label. Click **Finish**.

You will notice that you now have two fields on your form for **Style**. We need to delete the original **Style** field.

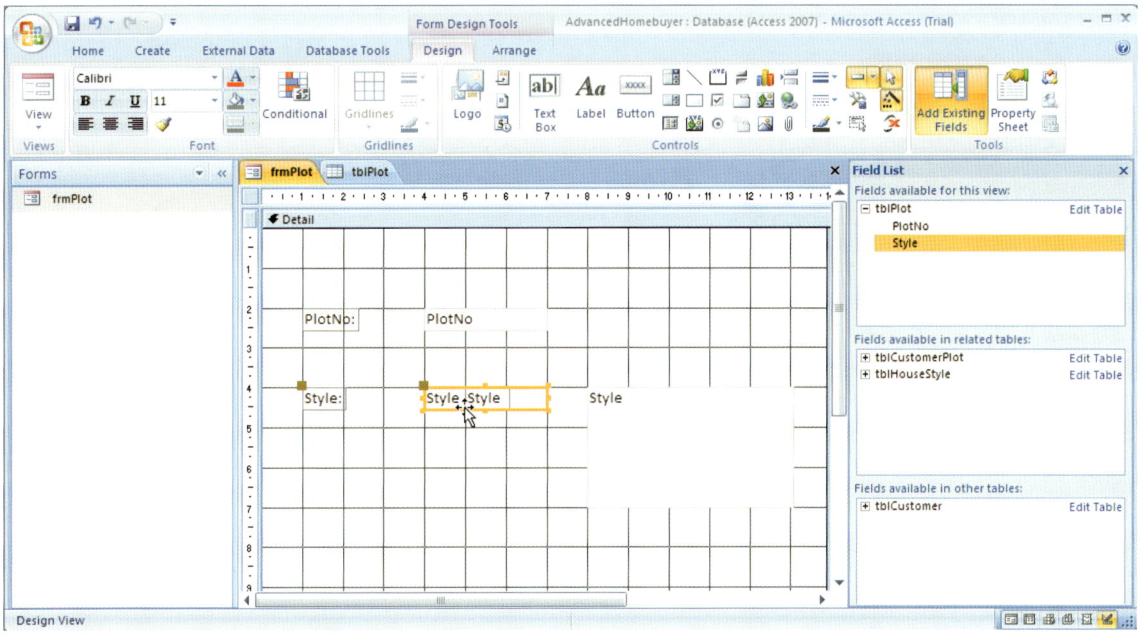

Figure 11.18

- Click on the original **Style** field to select it (make sure you click in the actual field, not its label). Click the **Delete** key.
- Now move the fields around until your form looks like Figure 11.19.

Tip:
You can move the label independently of its text or list box by clicking and dragging the large handle to the top left of the label.

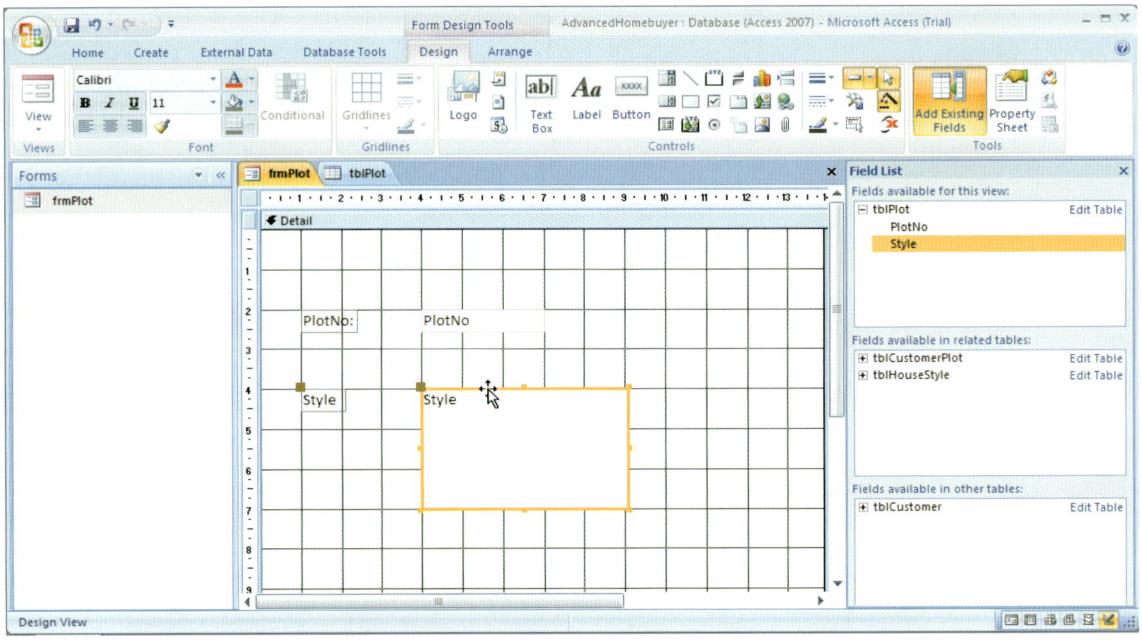

Figure 11.19

Command buttons

You are probably already familiar with the record selectors that appear at the bottom of the form (see Figure 11.20 for a reminder).

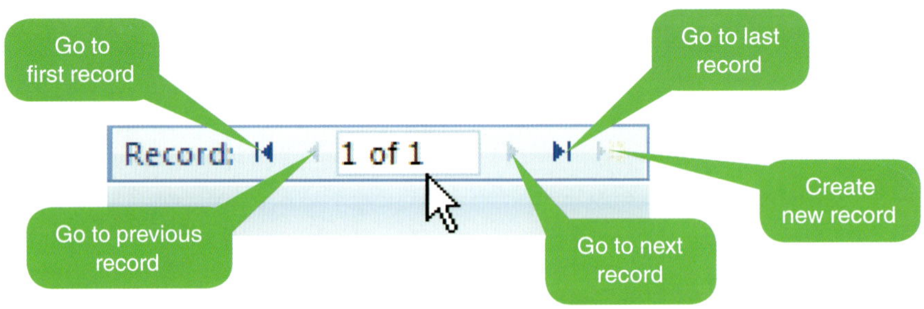

Figure 11.20

A nicer way to move between records in a form is to create your own buttons.

You can create buttons to do a variety of tasks. We will make one that opens a blank form ready for data to be entered.

▶ With your table in **Design View**, click the **Button Control** icon in the **Control** group on the **Design** tab.

Figure 11.21

- Click in an empty space on the form and drag out the shape you want for your button. (This can be adjusted later if you're not happy with it.)

The **Command Button Wizard** appears.

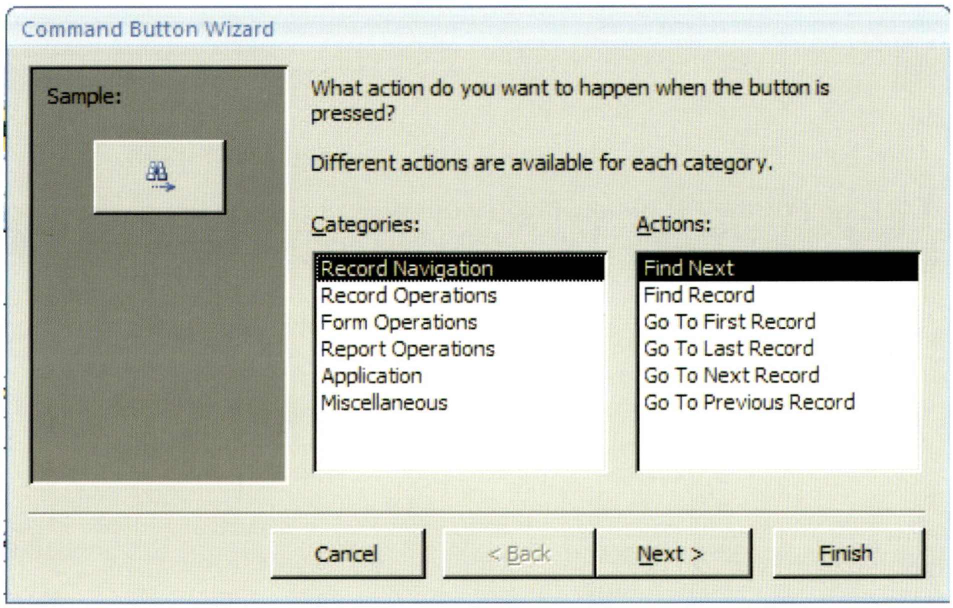

Figure 11.22

- Have a look at the wide variety of things which the **Command** buttons can do by clicking in turn on the entries in the **Categories** list, and looking at the **Actions** that appear on the right.
- Now click on **Record Operations** in the **Categories** box and **Add New Record** in the **Actions** box.
- Click **Next**.

You are now asked to choose whether you want **Text** or a **Picture** to appear on the button.

- We want the button to say **Enter New Plot**, so click in the box next to **Text**, and type **Enter New Plot**.

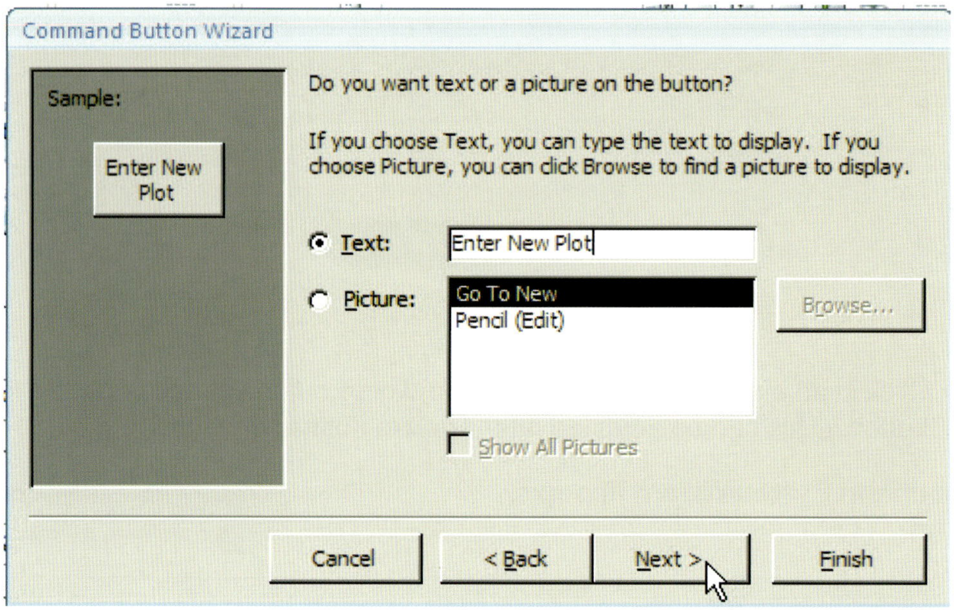

Figure 11.23

- Click **Next**. Name the button **NewPlotButton** and click **Finish**.
- Click the **Form View** button. If you would like to change the shape of your button return to **Design View** and click and drag the corners of the button.

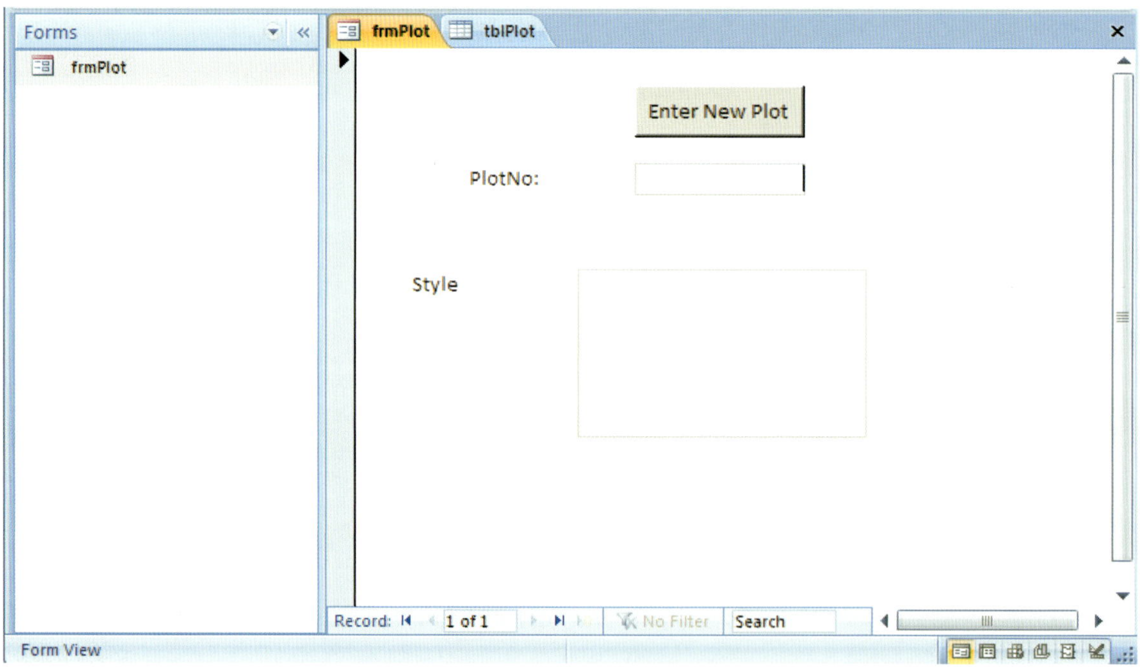

Figure 11.24

- When you are happy with the design, save and close the form.

Chapter 12 – Forms and Subforms

When this database is installed, the first thing to do will be to type in existing data about customers and the plots they are interested in. If you were typing in information about a customer who was interested in many plots, it would be convenient to type in all the information about the customer and the plots on the same form. To do this you need a form with a subform.

Subforms

Subforms are basically forms within forms. They are used when there is a **one-to-many** relationship.

In databases with a **one-to-many** relationship, the fields from the table on the one side would be on the main form, and the fields from the **many** side would appear on the subform.

Taking the example of the football team and player as the one-to-many relationship:

You would have the information about the football team on the main form, and within that would be a subform listing all the players within that team.

In this database we have three **one-to-many** relationships:

1. between **tblCustomer** and **tblCustomerPlot**
2. between **tblPlot** and **tblCustomerPlot**
3. between **tblHouseStyle** and **tblPlot**.

We have two options when creating a form to hold data about customers and plots they are interested in:

1. **Customer** could appear on the main form and the subform would contain all the plots that that customer was interested in, along with the stage of purchase and exchange date, etc.
2. **Plot** could appear on the main form and the subform would list all the customers who are interested in that plot.

We will create a form that fits the first option, because it is most likely that details of a plot will be entered before any customers are informed about it. When a new customer comes along their details will need to be entered together with the plot(s) they are interested in.

Creating the form

- Load Access and open the AdvancedHomebuyer database.
- Switch to the **Create** tab.

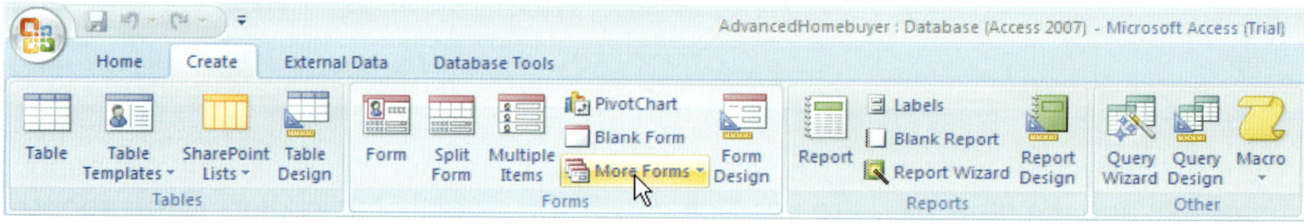

Figure 12.1

- Click the **More Forms** button and select **Form Wizard**
- In the **Form Wizard** window select **Table: tblCustomer** from the drop-down list.

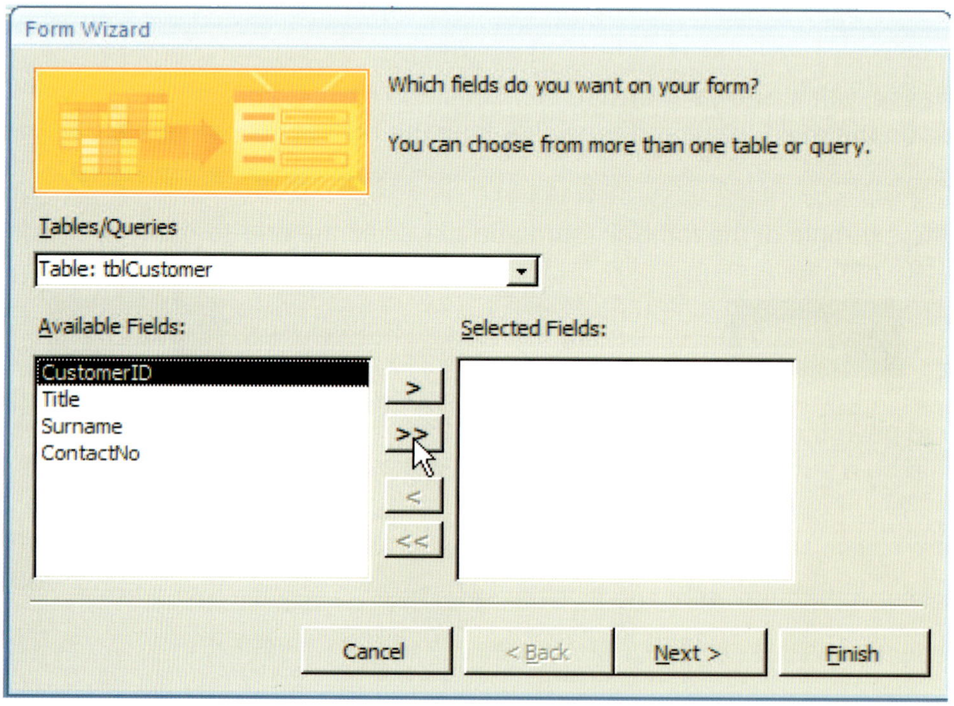

Figure 12.2

- We want all of the fields in **tblCustomer** to appear, so click **>>**

- Now select **Table: tblCustomerPlot** from the drop-down list.

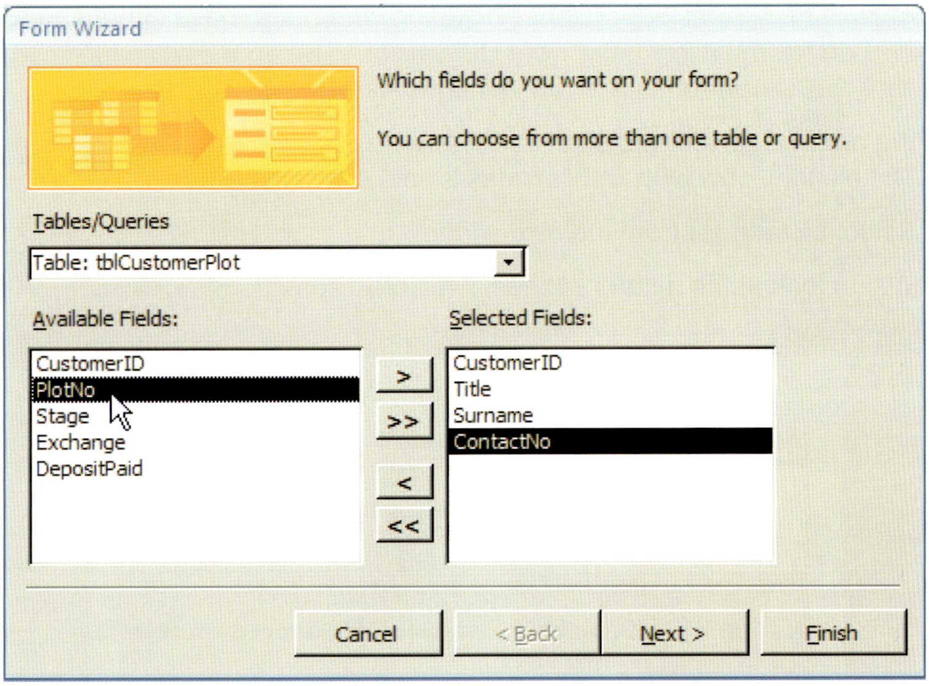

Figure 12.3

We want the fields **PlotNo**, **Stage**, **Exchange** and **DepositPaid** from this table.

- Select **PlotNo** and click >. Repeat this for the other fields mentioned above.
- Now select **Table: tblPlot** from the drop-down list.
- Select the field **Style** from **tblPlot**.
- Select the field **Price** from **tblHouseStyle**.
- Click **Next**.

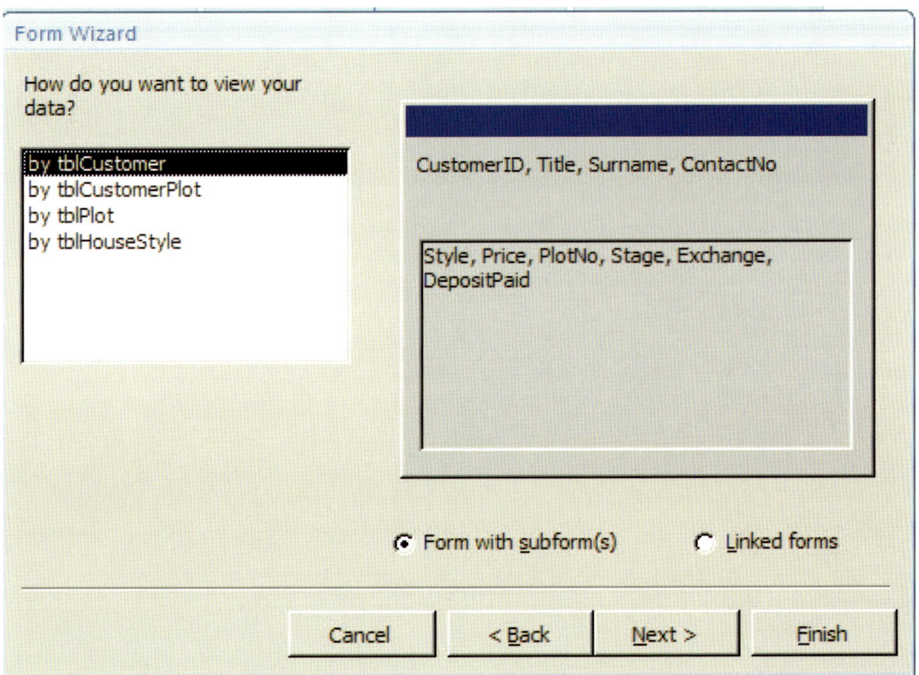

Figure 12.4

Note:
It is important that PlotNo is taken from tblCustomerPlot and not tblPlot. This is because tblCustomerPlot is the table that links the customer with the plots he or she is interested in. Details of the plots can be looked up in tblPlot.

- Access now gives four options, including whether to have either **Customer** or **Plot** on the main form. We want **Customer** to be on the main form, so make sure **tblCustomer** is selected in the box on the left.
- We are also given the option of **Form with subform(s)** or **Linked forms**. Make sure **Form with subform(s)** is selected and click **Next**.
- Select **Datasheet** from the next window and click **Next**.
- Take a look at the different styles available, then choose **Office**.

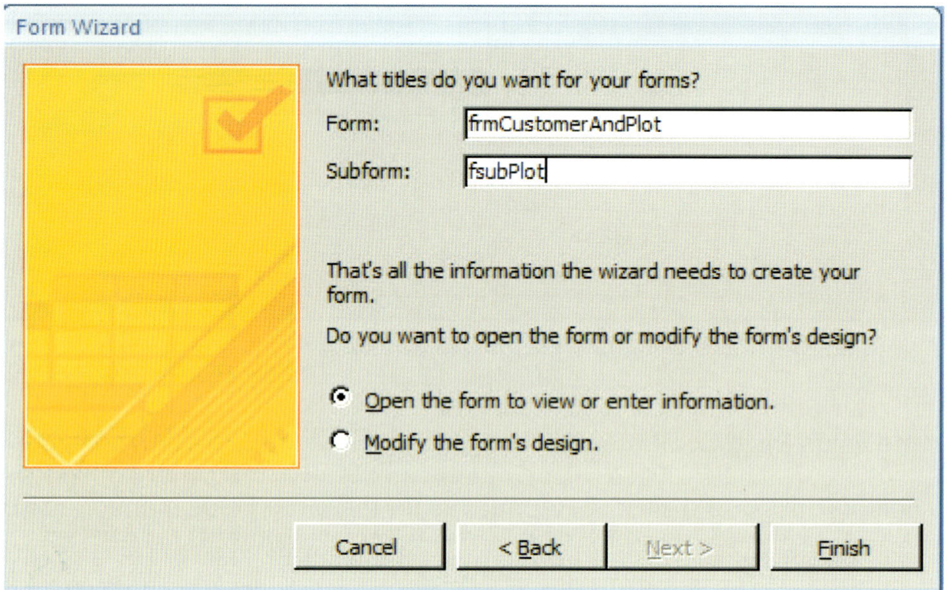

Figure 12.5

- Click **Next**. Save the form as **frmCustomerAndPlot** and the subform as **fsubPlot**.
- Click **Finish**.

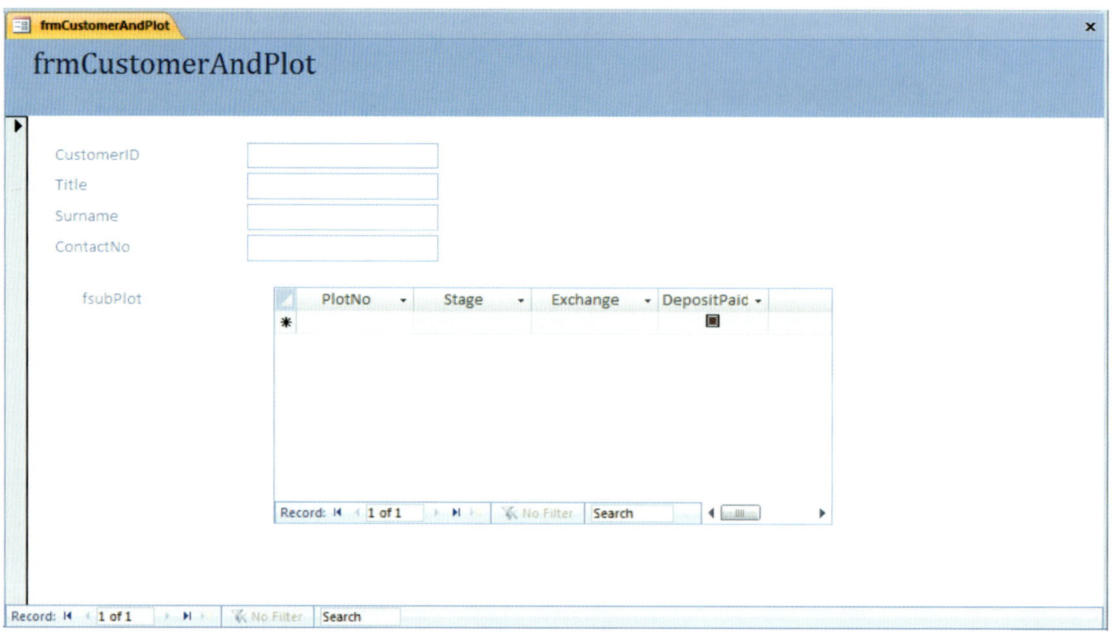

Figure 12.6

Editing the form

Now that you've created the form, there are a few things you need to do to make it look a bit more professional and user-friendly.

- Click the **View** button (**Home** tab) and select **Design View**.
- Close the **Shutter Bar** (**Navigation** pane) and the **Field List** (right-hand pane) to give you more room.
- First, delete the text in the label that says **fsubPlot**. Highlight the text and then press the **Delete** key.
- Highlight the subform by clicking on the top left corner square (see Figure 12.7).
- Minimise the label to give more room and lengthen the subform by clicking and dragging the orange handles.

Notice that the space given for the subform is slightly too small. Adjusting this so that it ends at the end of the **Price** field takes a bit of trial and error. You can move the whole subform in the main form's window using the cross arrow as shown in Figure 12.7.

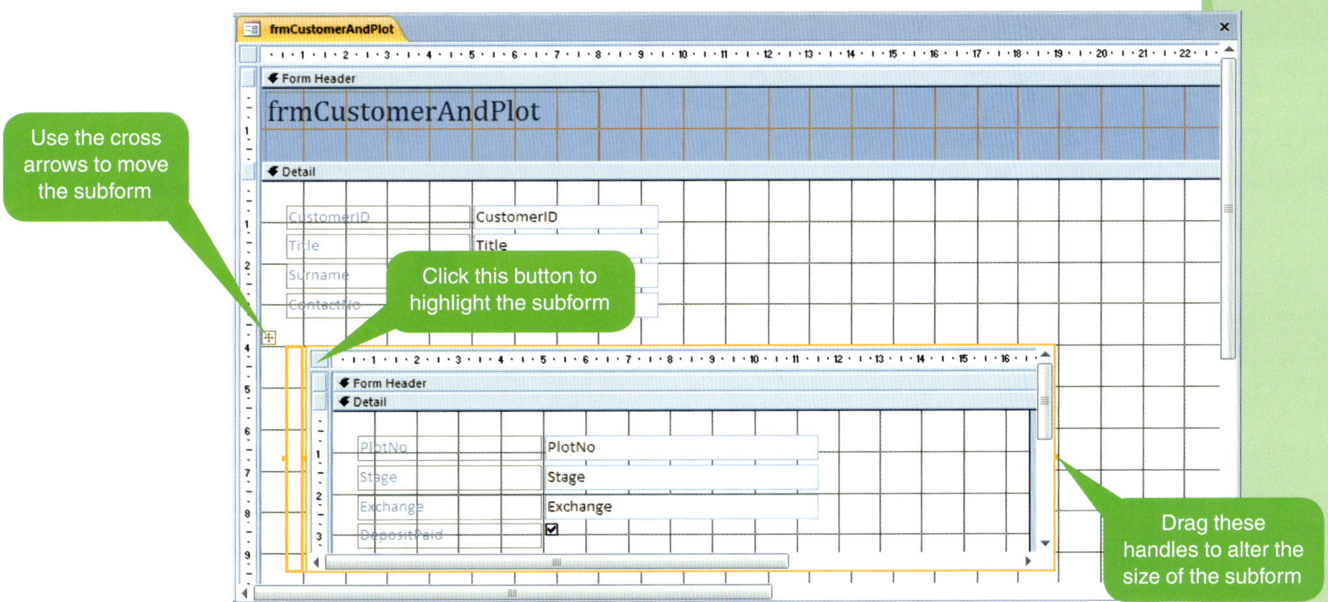

Figure 12.7

- Return to **Form View** to see if it is the right size – adjust this until you are happy with how it looks.

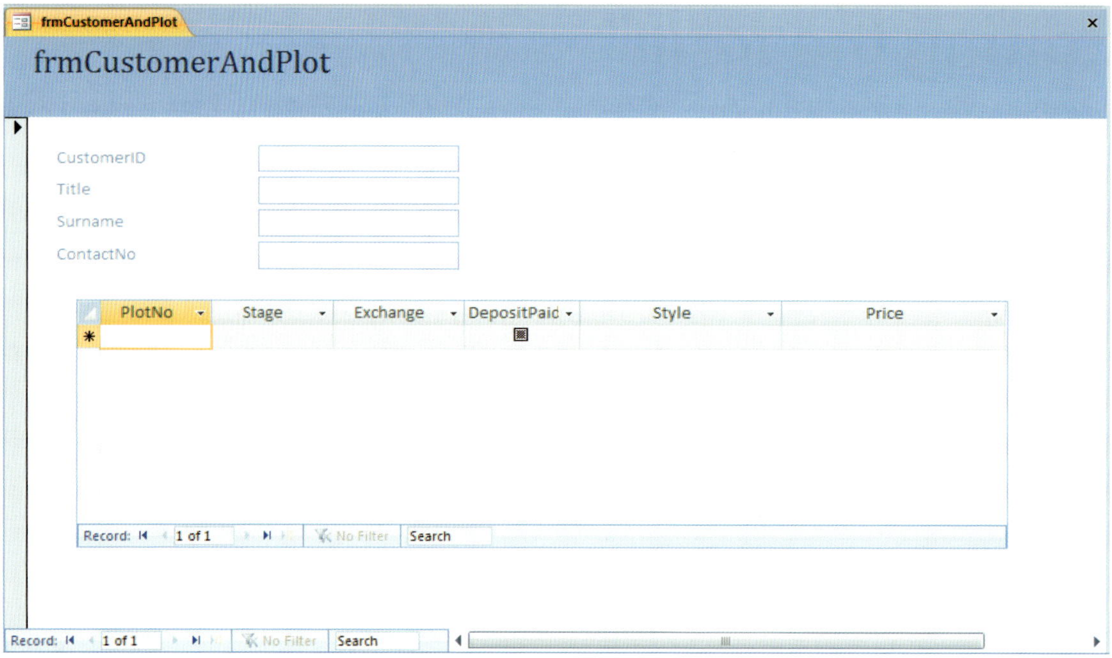

Figure 12.8

Making data entry quicker

Since there are only a set number of values of **PlotNo**, it would be convenient to select the plot number from a drop-down list. This would also ensure the sales staff didn't enter a **PlotNo** for a plot that hadn't been entered in the **tblPlot** table.

There are two options here:

- A **List box** shows a box on screen displaying some or all of the options (no drop-down list)

- A **Combo box** shows just one value at a time. To view all the options you click in the box to view the drop-down list.

Combo box

We will make the **PlotNo** field a **Combo box**.

- In **Design View**, click the **Combo Box** icon  and drag out a field in the **Detail** section on the subform. Make sure you click in the subform and not the main form.
- Select the option **I want the combo box to look up the values in a table or query**. Click **Next**.
- Select **tblPlot** in the next window. Click **Next**.

Select PlotNo and Style from the Available Fields. Click Next.

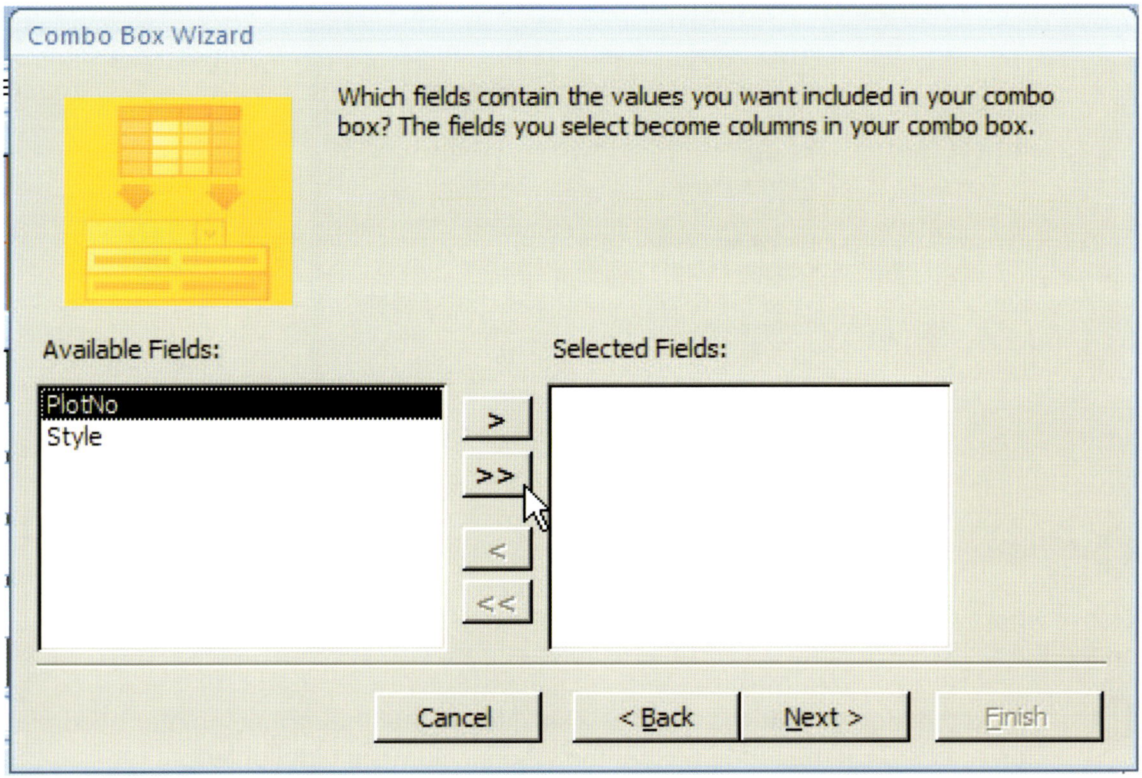

Figure 12.9

- Select PlotNo and Ascending and click Next.
- Deselect the check box marked Hide key column and click Next.
- Adjust the width of the fields to suit PlotNo and Style. Click Next.
- Select PlotNo from the next window. Click Next.
- Select Store that value in this field: and choose PlotNo from the drop-down list. Click Next.
- Save the combo box as PlotNo and click Finish.

Now look at the form in Form View. Notice that the original PlotNo field is still there, and the new one has been put right at the end. The original field needs to be deleted and the new one put in its place.

- In Design View, click the original PlotNo field and click the Delete key.
- Right click the new field and select Properties from the menu.
- Make sure the All tab is selected in the Properties box, and change the Name field from Combo14 to PlotNo.

Tip:
With a list box you can only select a value from a list. With a combo box, you can either select a value or type in a new one.

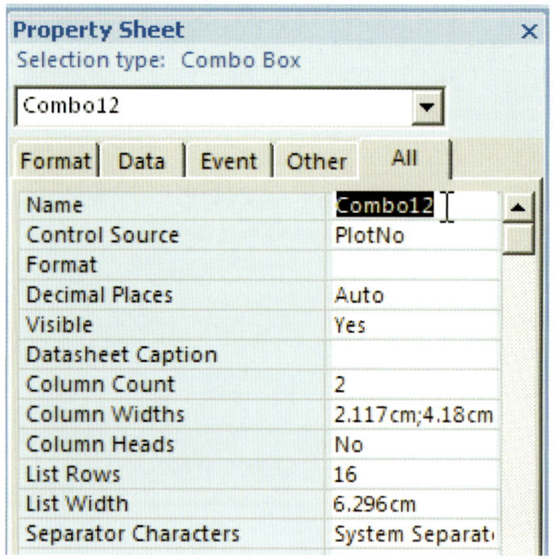

Figure 12.10

- Go to **Form View**.

This is where we'll change the position of the **PlotNo** field back to its original location on the form.

- Hold the mouse over the **PlotNo** label. Notice that the mouse pointer becomes an arrow. Click the label, so that the whole column is highlighted.
- Now click and drag the label over to the left of the **Stage** field, and drop it.
- Adjust the width of the new **PlotNo** field so that all the fields fit on the subform.

The field should now be on the far left (Figure 12.11):

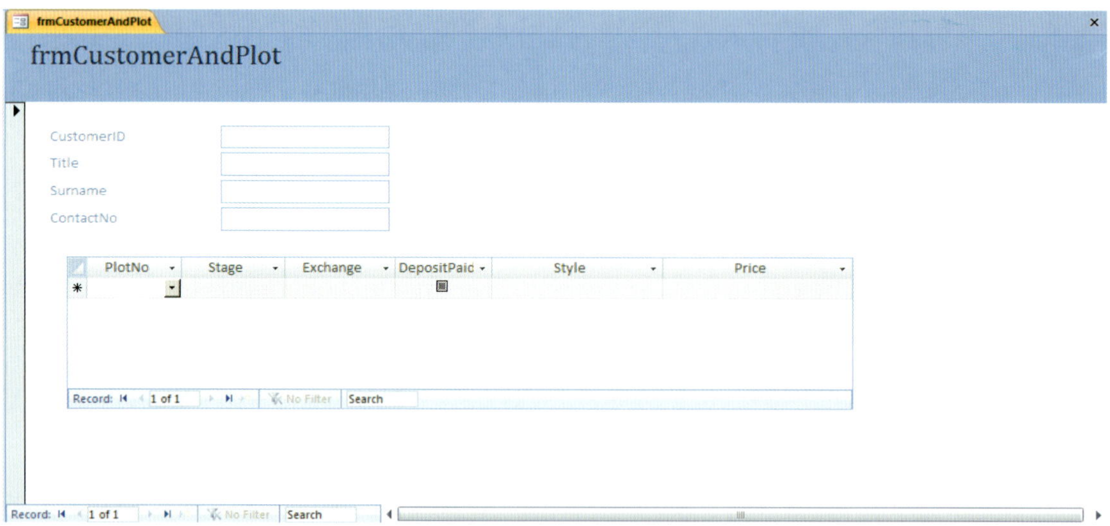

Figure 12.11

It would also be useful to make the **Stage** field a combo box. Use the same method to create another combo box on the subform for the **Stage** field. Type in the four stages (**Interested**, **Reserved**, **Exchanged**, **Completed**) and save the value of that field to **Stage**. Remember to delete the original stage field. Save your combo box as **Stage** and make sure it appears in the correct position in **Form View**.

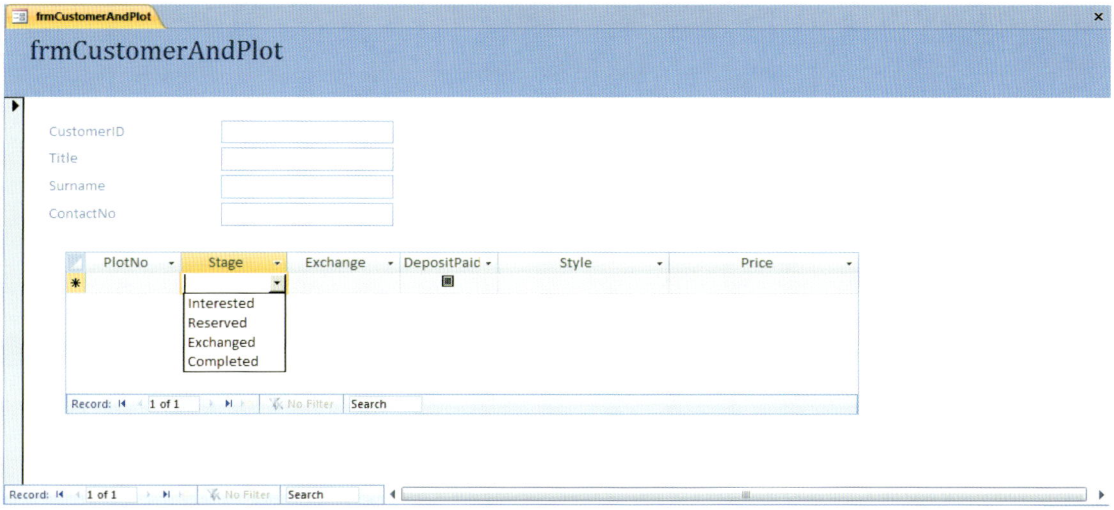

Figure 12.12

Tab order

When you start entering data using your form, the cursor should automatically be positioned in the first field, and when you click **Tab** (the key to the left of **Q** on the keyboard) the cursor should go to the next field. If you have entered extra fields on your form when designing it, the cursor may jump to an unexpected place when you click **Tab**.

Before starting the data entry, make sure that the **Tab Order** is the way you like it on both forms by tabbing through the fields in Form view. If it is not correct, go to the **Arrange** tab of the **Ribbon** while in **Design View**, and click the **Tab Order** button. To edit the tab order of the subform, click on a field in the subform to highlight it first.

You may find that some of the fields are called something like **List18**. You can change this by right clicking on the field in **Design View** and changing the name in the **Properties** box.

- When you are happy with the tab order, save and close the form.

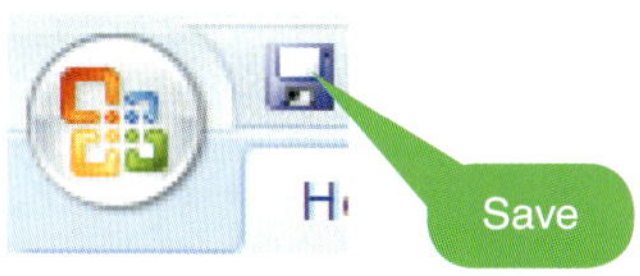

Figure 12.13

Data entry

Before using your new forms, you can enter some data directly into the **tblHouseStyle** table.

- Open **tblHouseStyle** from the Database window.
- Enter all the house styles and prices as in Figure 12.14.
- Close the table when you are finished.

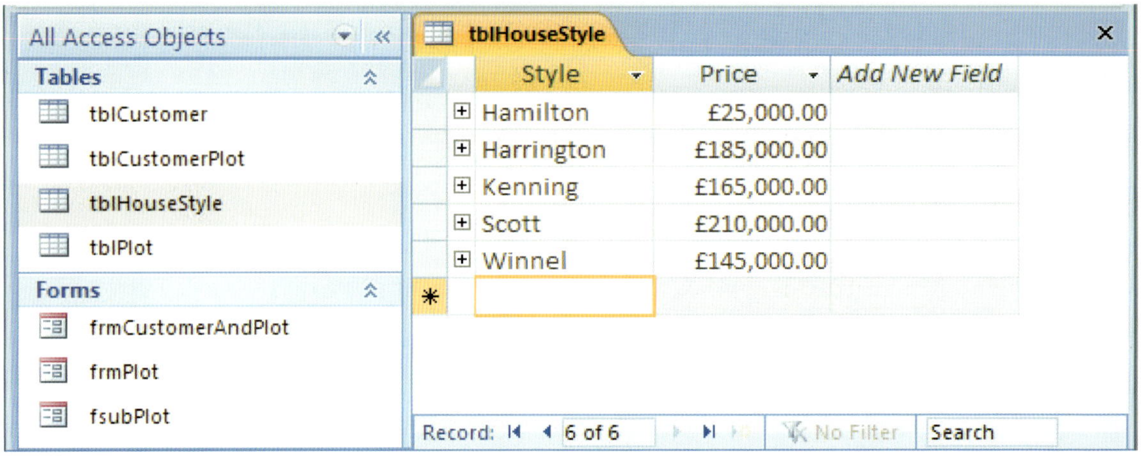

Figure 12.14

OK, it's time to use the forms.

First enter the plots:

- Open **frmPlot** from the Database window.
- Enter the plots listed in Table 12.1.

Tip:
For each new record, use your Enter New Plot button instead of the record selectors!

PlotNo	PlotStyle
1	Kenning
2	Winnel
3	Scott
4	Hamilton
5	Harrington
6	Harrington
7	Scott
8	Winnel
9	Harrington
10	Kenning
11	Hamilton
12	Winnel
13	Harrington

Table 12.1

- When you have entered all the plots, close **frmPlot**. The data is automatically saved as you enter it, so you won't be prompted to save anything unless you've changed the form in **Design View**.

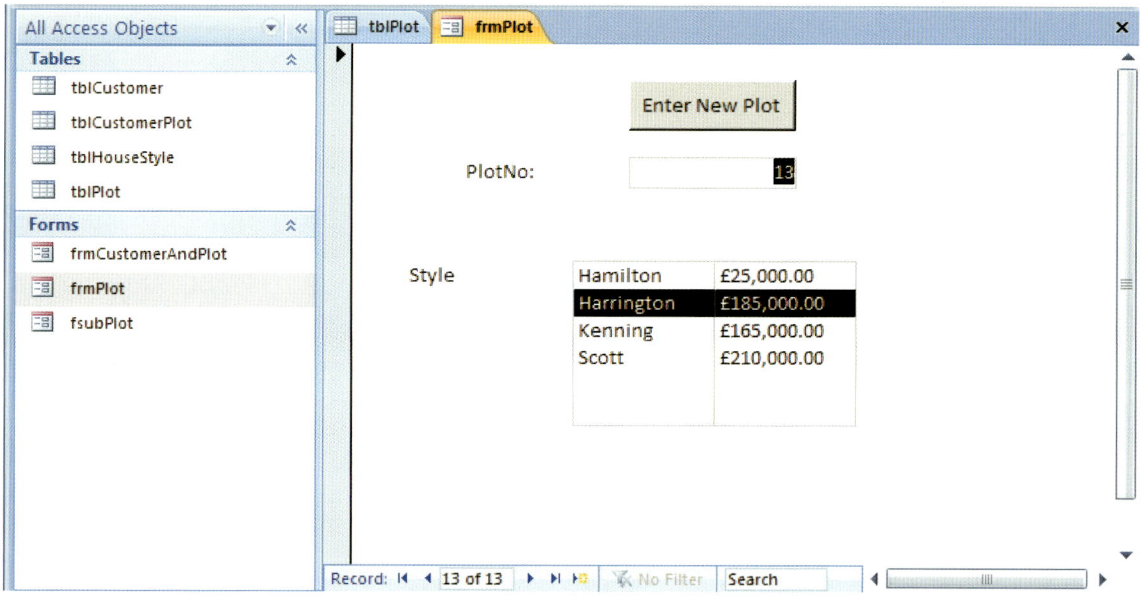

Figure 12.15

Now we will use the **frmCustomerAndPlot** form to enter a list of existing customers and the plots they are interested in.

- Open **frmCustomerAndPlot**.
- Enter the first customer from Table 12.2, **Mr Hainsworth**, along with his personal details.

Now look at the last column in the table, which lists the **PlotNo** of each plot he is interested in.

- Click in the **PlotNo** field in the subform. Select the row with **PlotNo 5** from the list that appears.

Notice that the other plot details are automatically filled in. The **Stage** field will automatically say **Interested** because we set that as the default value.

- Repeat this for the second plot, **PlotNo 9**.

CustomerID	Title	Surname	ContactNo	PlotNos of Prospective Plots
201	Mr	Hainsworth	01474 678456	5 (interested) 9 (interested)
202	Mr	Hodson	01474 212394	1 (interested)
203	Mr	Stevenson	01474 665498	3 (reserved, exchange 1/12/2007, deposit Y)
204	Miss	Hart	01474 374509	5 (interested) 13 (interested)
205	Mr	Ellis	01474 151884	2 (exchanged 15/08/2007, deposit Y)
206	Mrs	Harris	01474 908635	4 (reserved, exchange 3/12/2007, deposit Y) 11 (interested)
207	Mr	Iqbal	01474 673028	6 (reserved, exchange 7/12/2007, deposit Y)
208	Miss	Jones	01474 255836	1 (interested) 8 (interested) 10 (interested)
209	Mr	Harris	01474 682453	5 (interested)

Table 12.2

Enter all the other customers and plots from Table 12.2.

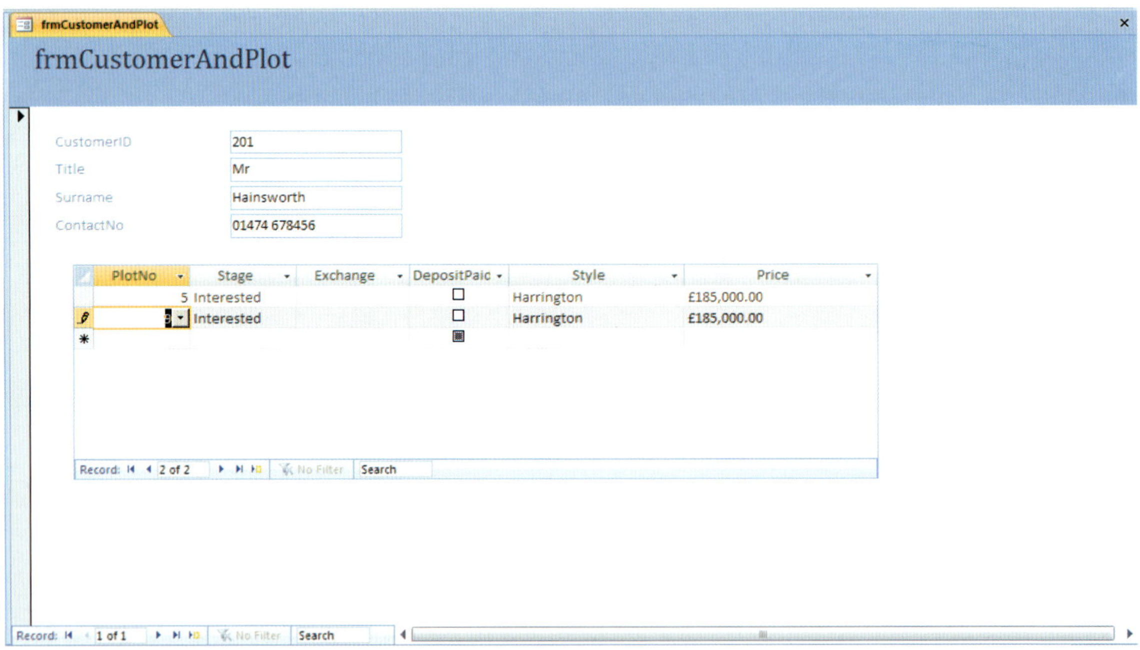

Figure 12.16

When all the data has been entered, close the form.

Chapter 13 – Advanced Queries

We will now design some queries that will help find customers who may be interested in particular plots.

For example, we could search for:

- all customers who have registered an interest in plots of a particular house style
- all customers who are interested in plots of a particular price range.

We will make a query which allows us to search for customers who are interested in a particular house style. In order to do this the query will contain all tables except the **tblHouseStyle** table.

New query

- Open the **AdvancedHomebuyer** database and swap to the **Create** tab to select **Queries** on the **Ribbon**.

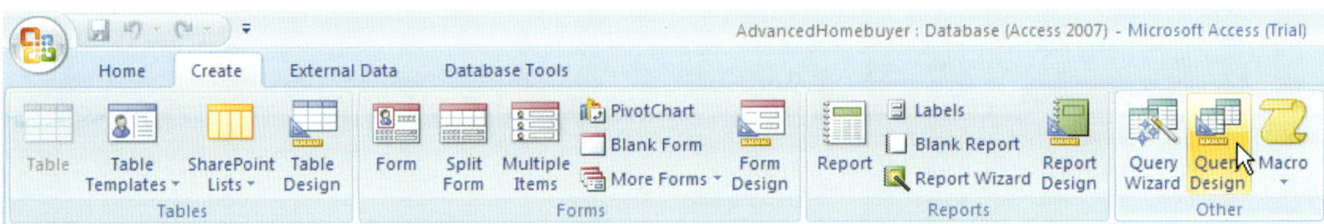

Figure 13.1

- click the **Query Design** button.

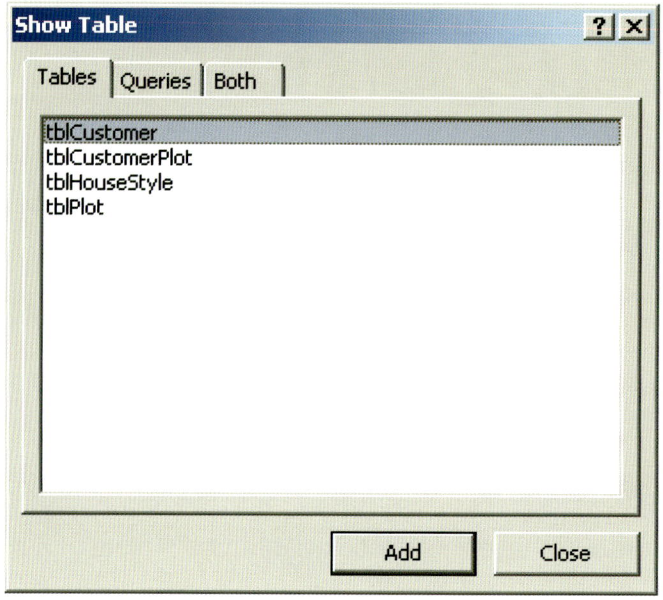

Figure 13.2

- Select **tblCustomer** and click **Add**. Repeat this for **tblCustomerPlot** and **tblPlot**.
- Click **Close**.
- We want all the fields from the **tblCustomer** table to appear in the query, so double click each one in turn, and watch as they appear in the query grid in the bottom half of the window.

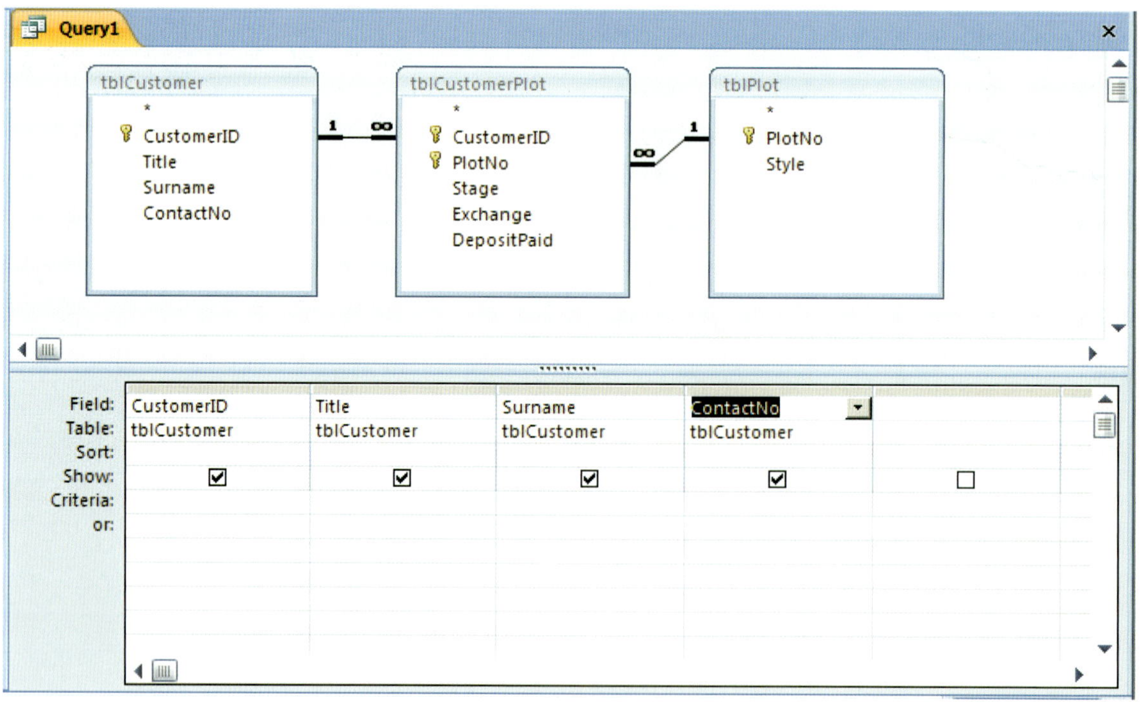

Figure 13.3

- Add **Stage** from **tblCustomerPlot**.
- Add **Style** from **tblPlot**.

We'd like the query results sorted by **Surname**, so set the **Sort** row of the **Surname** column to **Ascending**.

Adding criteria

We would like the query to return a list of every customer who is interested in a **Kenning**.

- In the **Criteria** row of the **Stage** column enter **Interested**.
- In the **Criteria** row of the **Style** column, type **Kenning**.
- Test the query by clicking the **Run** button.

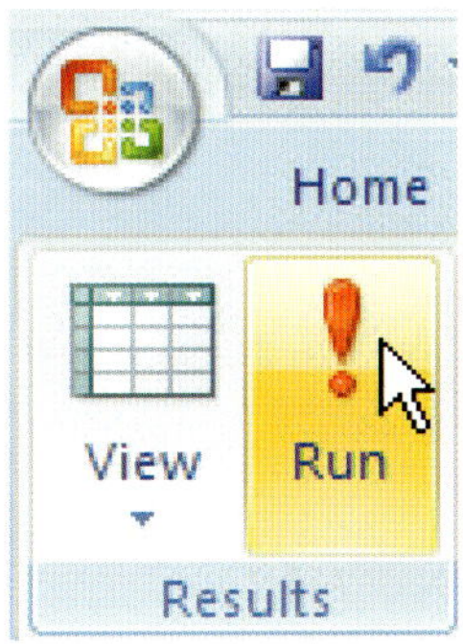

Your query should look like Figure 13.4.

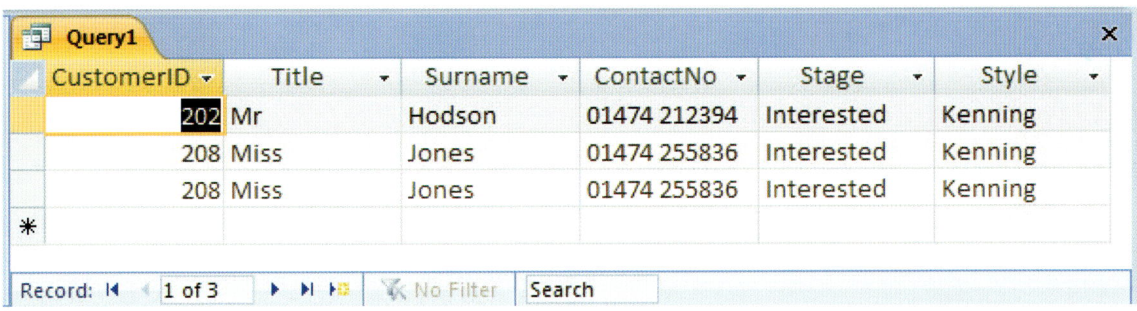

Query1

CustomerID	Title	Surname	ContactNo	Stage	Style
202	Mr	Hodson	01474 212394	Interested	Kenning
208	Miss	Jones	01474 255836	Interested	Kenning
208	Miss	Jones	01474 255836	Interested	Kenning
*					

Record: 1 of 3 No Filter Search

Figure 13.4

Notice that **Miss Jones**'s record appears twice – we don't want this. To make sure no record appears twice just follow the instructions below:

- Switch to **Design View**.

- Right click anywhere in the query design view outside the design grid and the field lists.
- Select **Properties** from the drop-down menu.
- On the query's property sheet set the **Unique Values** property to **Yes**.

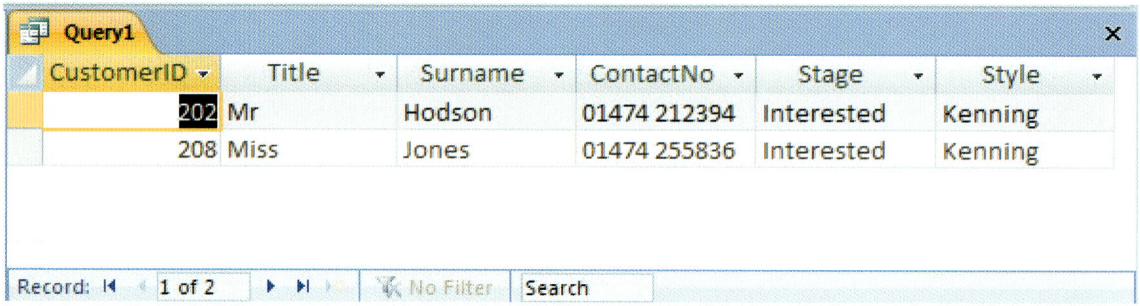

Query1

CustomerID	Title	Surname	ContactNo	Stage	Style
202	Mr	Hodson	01474 212394	Interested	Kenning
208	Miss	Jones	01474 255836	Interested	Kenning

Record: 1 of 2 No Filter Search

Figure 13.5

- Now run the query again to check that it has worked.

Allowing the user to enter criteria

Since we will want to look at other styles of house besides Kenning, it would be useful if we can specify the house style every time we run the query.

This is really straightforward:

- Return to the query design by clicking the **Design View** icon.

In the **Criteria** row in the **Style** column delete **Kenning** and enter **[Please enter house style]**, don't omit the square brackets (to the left of **Enter**).

To show what this does, we'll run the query:

Click the **Run** button on the menu bar.

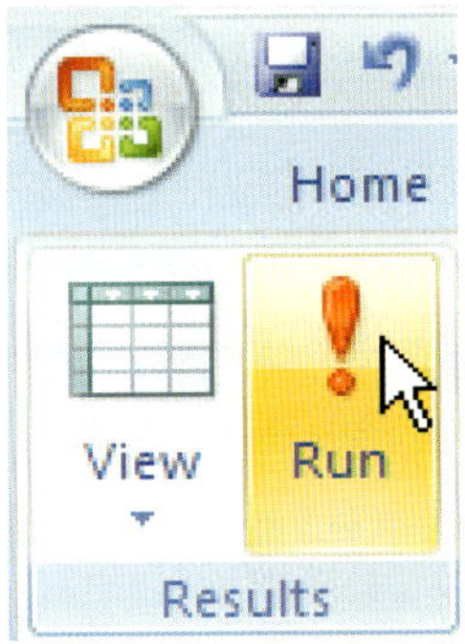

A window appears with the message you typed.

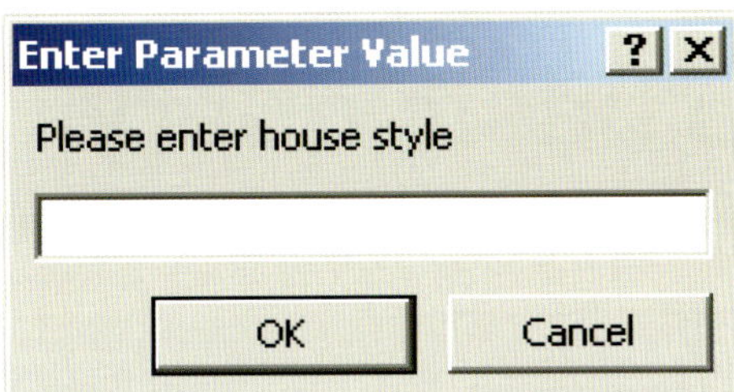

Figure 13.6

Enter **Harrington** and click **OK**.

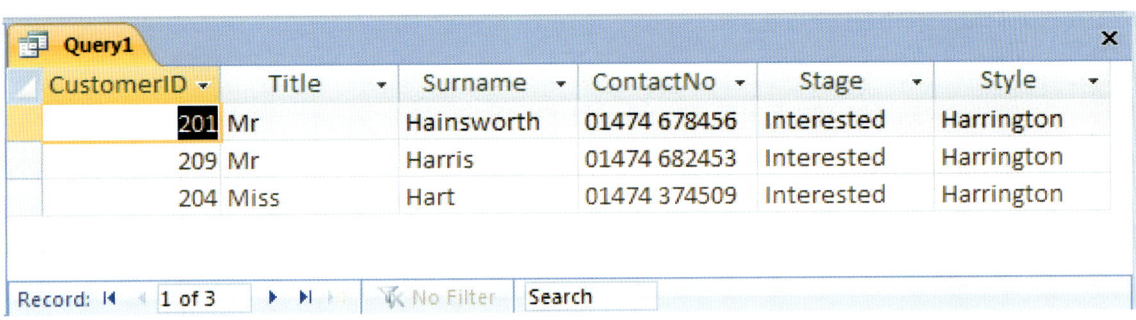

Query1

CustomerID	Title	Surname	ContactNo	Stage	Style
201	Mr	Hainsworth	01474 678456	Interested	Harrington
209	Mr	Harris	01474 682453	Interested	Harrington
204	Miss	Hart	01474 374509	Interested	Harrington

Record: 1 of 3 No Filter Search

Figure 13. 7

Three records should be returned from the query as shown in Figure 13.7.

Save the query as **qryHouseStyle** then close it.

Chapter 14 – Reports

Reports are useful for presenting query results in a more professional way, but they also have other useful features. Reports allow you to display sum or average fields, or do almost any other arithmetic operation on numeric fields.

We will use the **Count** function to give a summary of how many customers have or will exchange contracts each month during a specified period.

First of all, we need to create a query that will select all the records where the exchange date falls in the specified period.

Creating the basic query

- Swap to the **Create** tab and click the **Query Design** button.

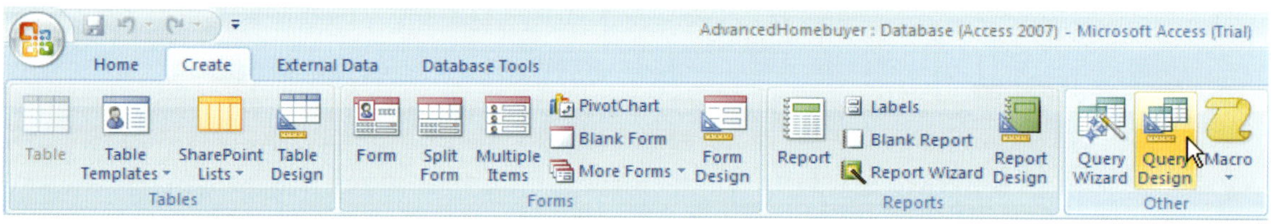

Figure 14.1

- Select **tblCustomer** and click **Add**. Add **tblCustomerPlot** in the same way.
- Close this window by clicking the **Close** button.
- Double click the fields **Title**, **Surname** and **ContactNo** from **tblCustomer**.
- Add the fields **Stage** and **Exchange** from **tblCustomerPlot**.

They should appear in the query grid as shown in Figure 14.2:

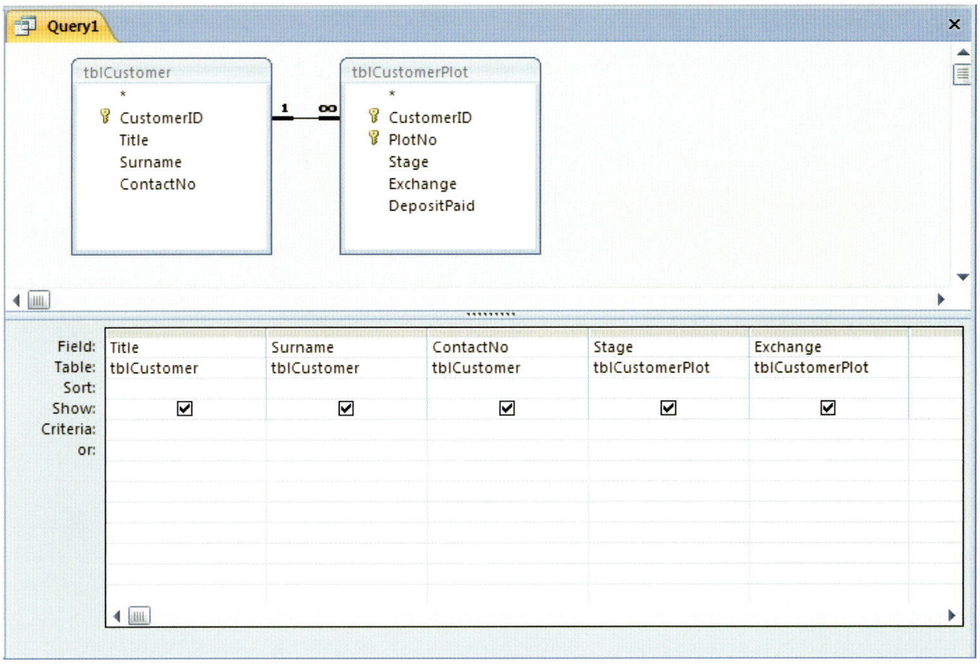

Figure 14.2

- Type **Between [Enter start date] And [Enter end date]** as the criteria in the **Exchange** column.
- Run the query to check that it works.

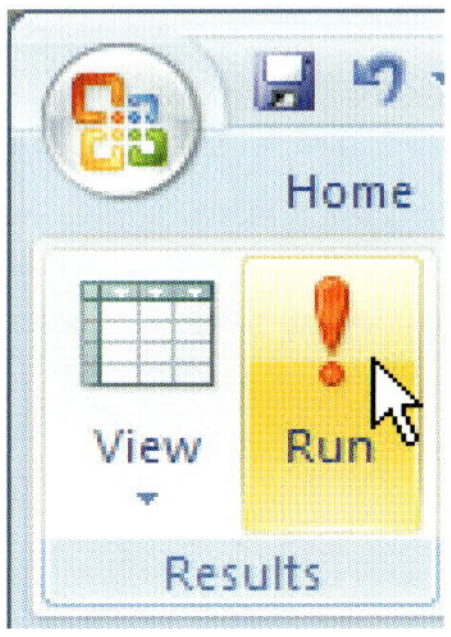

- Save the query as **qryExchangeInPeriod** and close the query.

Creating the report

The report will be based on the query we have just created, **qryExchangeInPeriod**.

- Swap to the **Create** tab and click the **Report Wizard** button.

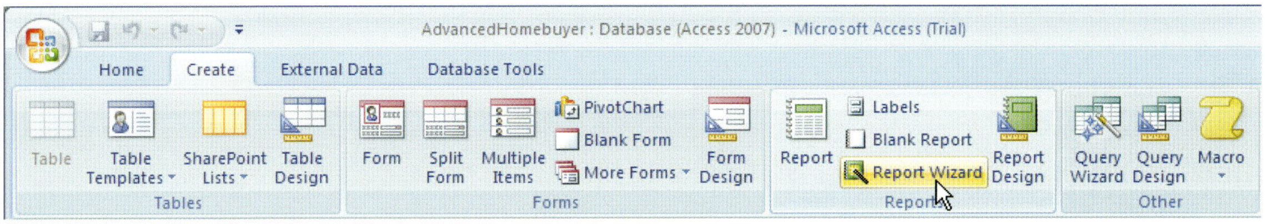

Figure 14.3

Select **Report Wizard** from the list of options, and choose **qryExchangeInPeriod** from the drop-down list.

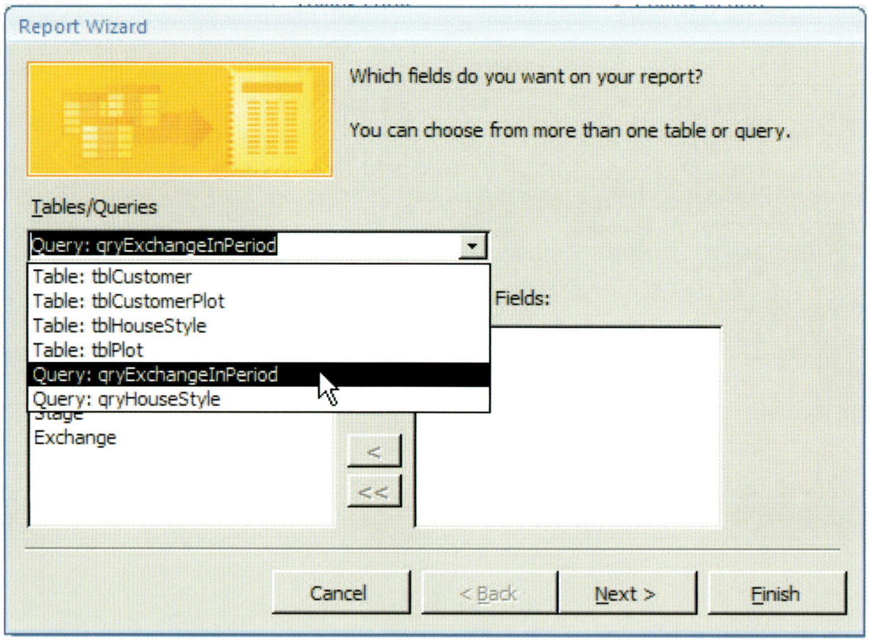

Figure 14.4

We would like all of the fields to appear in the query so click >>. These fields will appear in the right-hand pane.

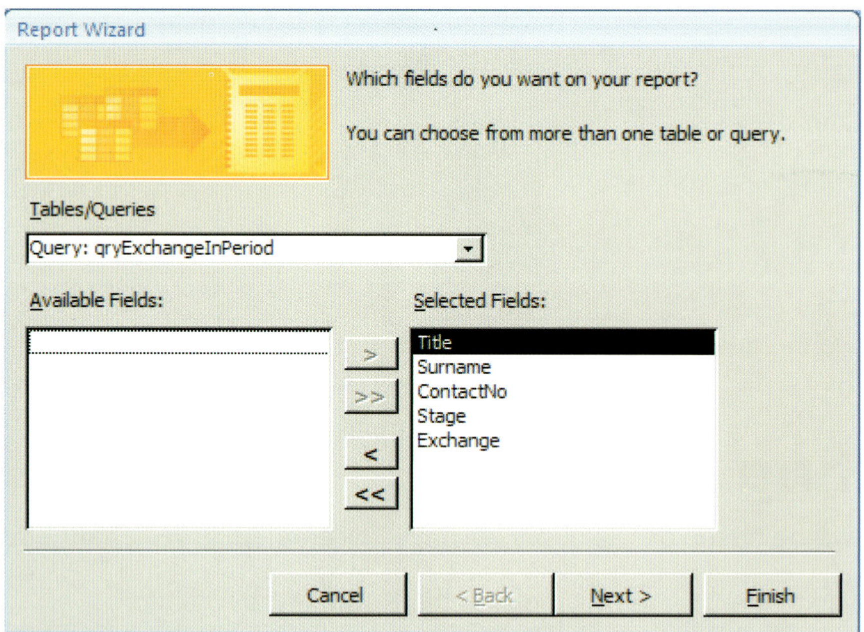

Figure 14.5

Click **Next**.

The next window asks how you would like to view your data.

Select **tblCustomerPlot** from the left-hand pane. Click **Next**.

You are now asked to add grouping levels. Since we would like to see which plots will exchange each month, we would like **Exchange** to be the first grouping level.

- Select **Exchange** and click >. **Exchange by Month** should now appear at the top of the page.

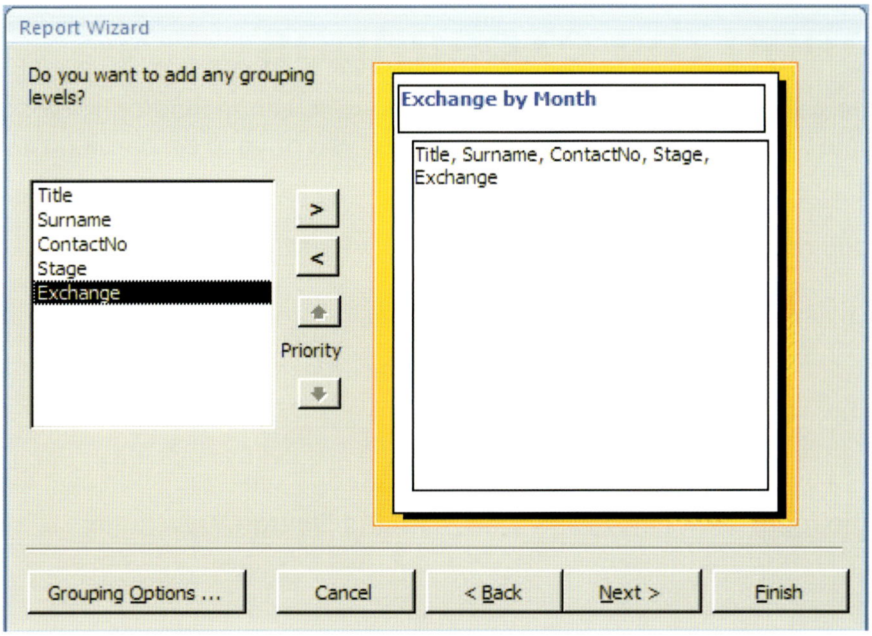

Figure 14.6

- Click **Next**. Select **Exchange** from the first drop-down list to sort the records in order of exchange date. Select **Stage** from the second drop-down list. Click **Next**.
- The next two windows ask about the format of the report. You can try out some different styles, otherwise just click **Next** in each window.
- Save the report as **rptExchangeInPeriod** and click **Finish**.

You are now asked for the start and end date of the report.

- Enter **1/1/2007** and **1/1/2008** as the start and end dates.

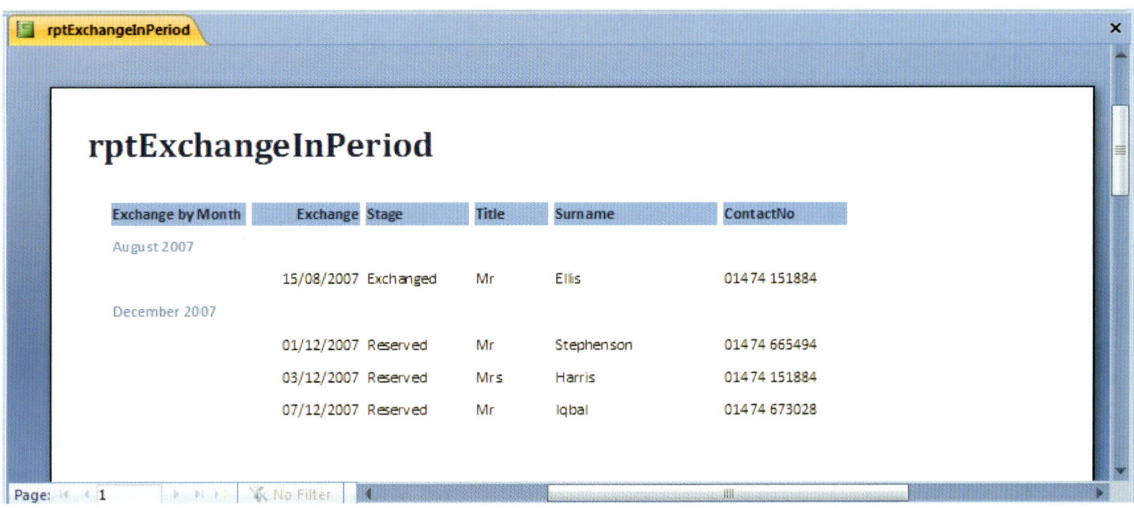

Figure 14.7

You have now created the basic report! Now we need to add fields which count the number of exchanges each month, and also add a total number of exchanges over the selected period. These totalling fields would be much more useful to the sales staff when there are many more customers and exchanges.

Counting the exchanges

To do this we will add a field in the **Exchange Header**. When inserting fields that add up or do some other maths operation on a report, you have to be careful which section of the report the field is put in.

- Go to report design by clicking the **Close Print Preview** button.

- If the report is not in Design View, click the **Design View** button.

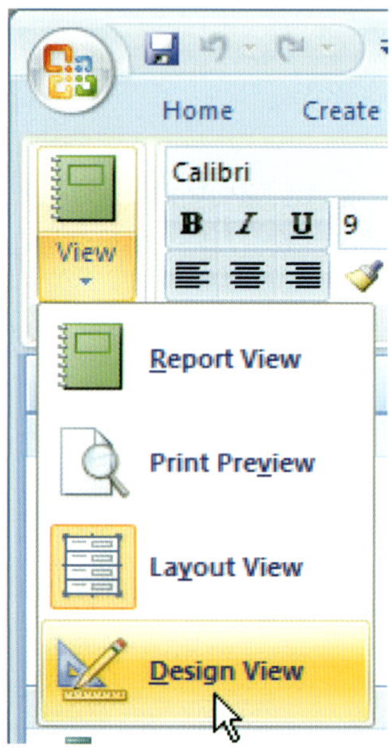

Figure 14.8

- Click the button for the **Text Box** control in **Report Design Tools**, **Design** tab, and click once under the **Exchange Header**, which will create a default sized text box and its associated label.

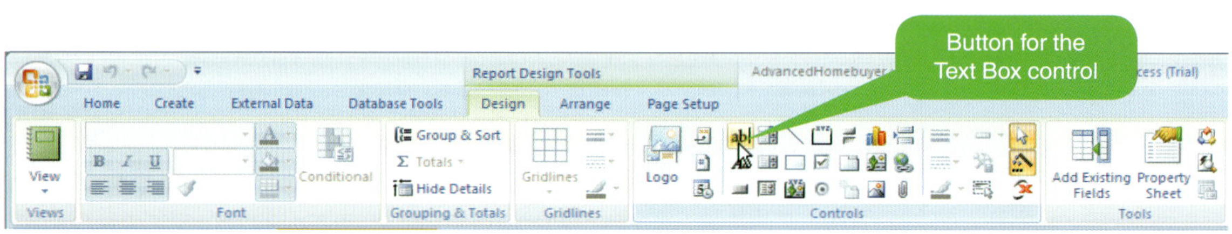

Figure 14.9

Click in the field where it says **Unbound**. The word **Unbound** disappears; now type **=Count(Exchange)**.

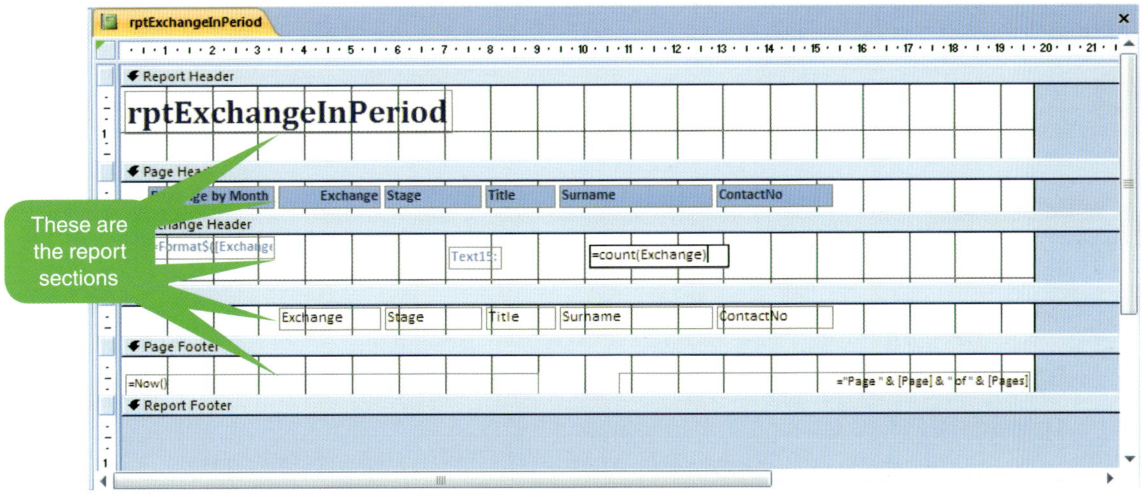

Figure 14.10

Now see if this works by clicking the **Print Preview** button.

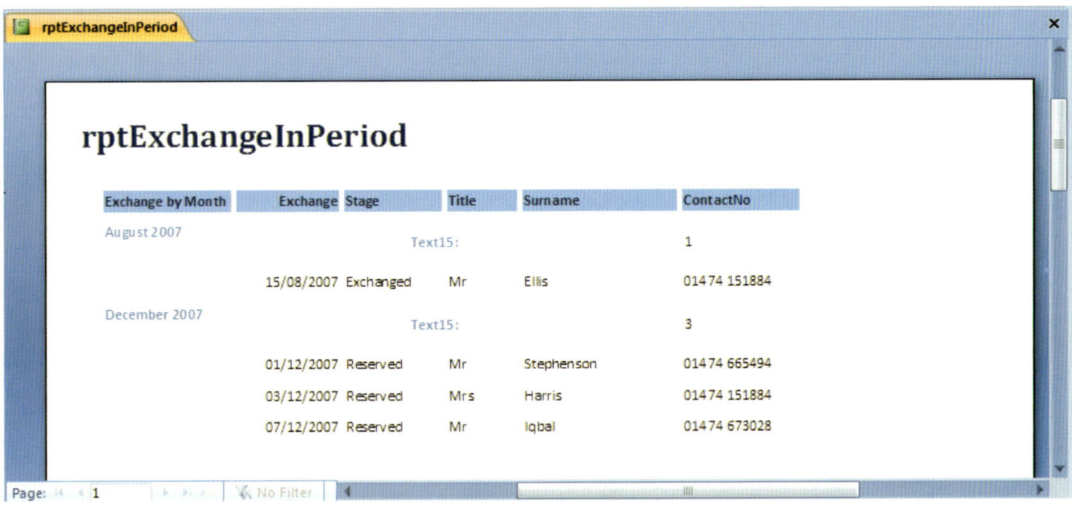

Figure 14.11

That seems to work! Now we will add one more field to total all the exchanges in the report, then we will do some tidying up.

Return to **Design View**.

To get a total for the whole report, we need to add a field in the **Report Footer**. In fact, we can put in exactly the same expression we did before, but because it is in a different section on the report, it will give a different total!

Click on the field you created above:
=Count([Exchange])

Now right click and select **Copy** on the **Shortcut** menu.

Note:
Access will add square brackets around the field that you are performing the function on upon exiting from the text box.

Click on the bar named **Report Footer**, then right click and select **Paste** from the **Shortcut** menu.

The same field should appear. Now we want to rename the labels and make sure the fields appear in the right place.

In **Design View**, change the labels of both the fields you have just created to look like Figure 14.12. Change the report heading to **Exchange Report**.

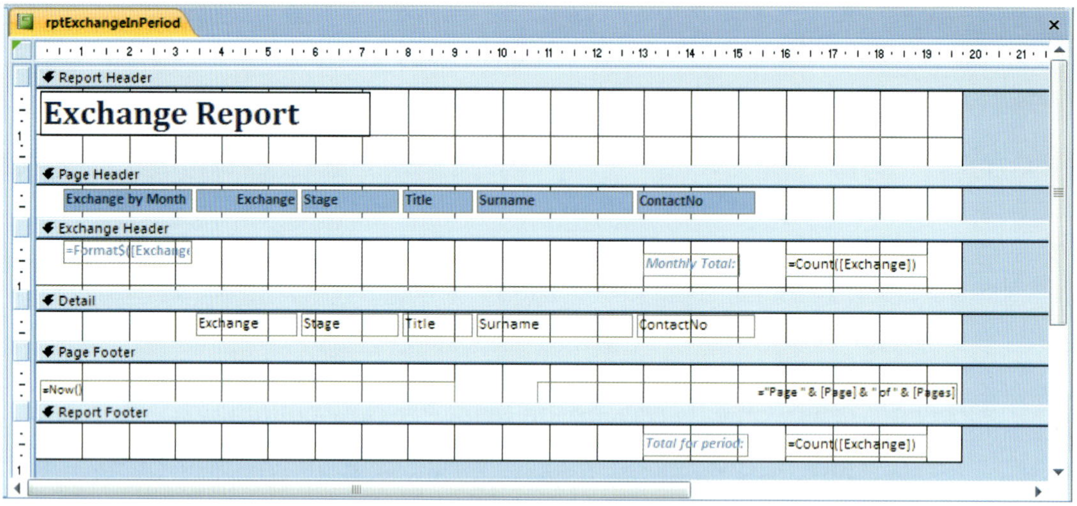

Figure 14.12

Now test the report by clicking the **Print Preview** button.

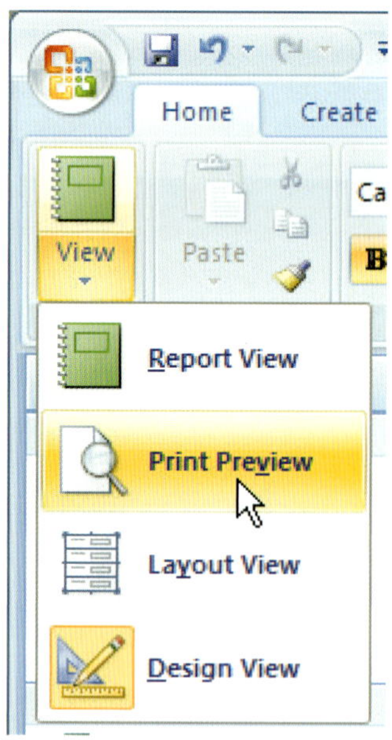

Figure 14.13

Exchange footer

Suppose you wanted the subtotals below each list of customers instead of above them. You would do this by moving the **Count** field to the **Exchange Footer** from the **Exchange Header**. Notice that there is no **Exchange Footer** on your report – the first step is to add this.

- Click the **Group & Sort** button on the **Report Design Tools**, **Design** tab.

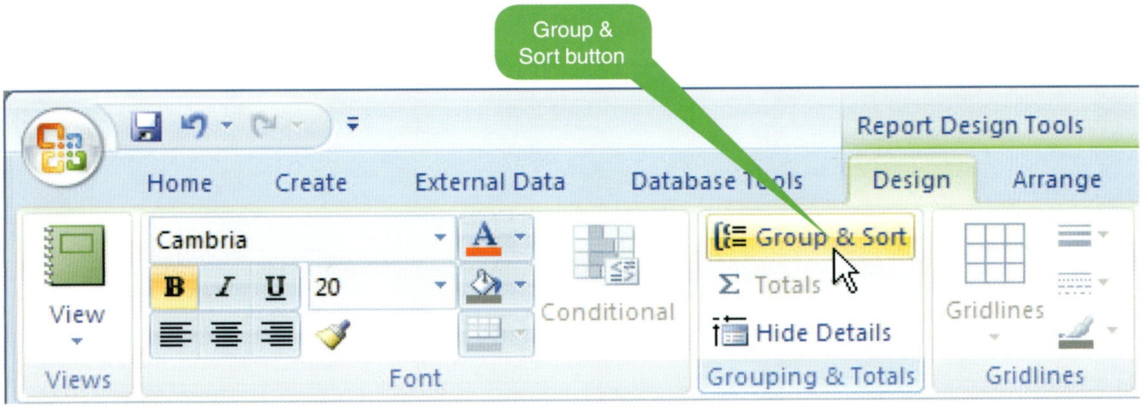

Figure 14.14

- The **Sorting and Grouping** window appears at the bottom of the screen. In the top **Group on Exchange** click **More** to reveal all of the options and change **without a footer section** to **with a footer section**; see Figure 14.15:

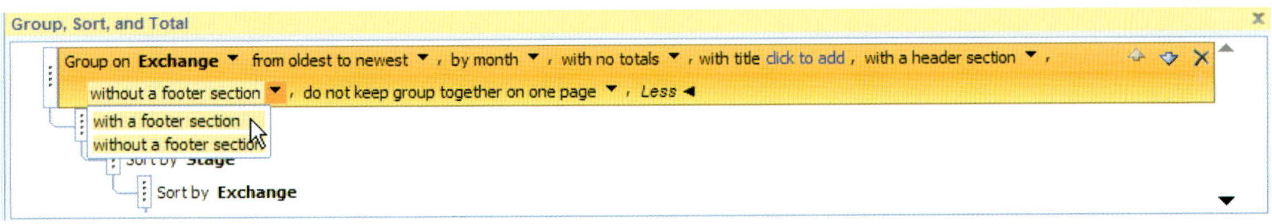

Figure 14.15

- Close the window. You will notice that there is now a section labelled **Exchange Footer** on the report.
- Click and drag the **Count** field that is currently in the **Exchange Header** to the **Exchange Footer**.
- Run the report.

Reminder:
The field name you write in the text box is the same as you wrote in square brackets in qryExchangeIn-Period.

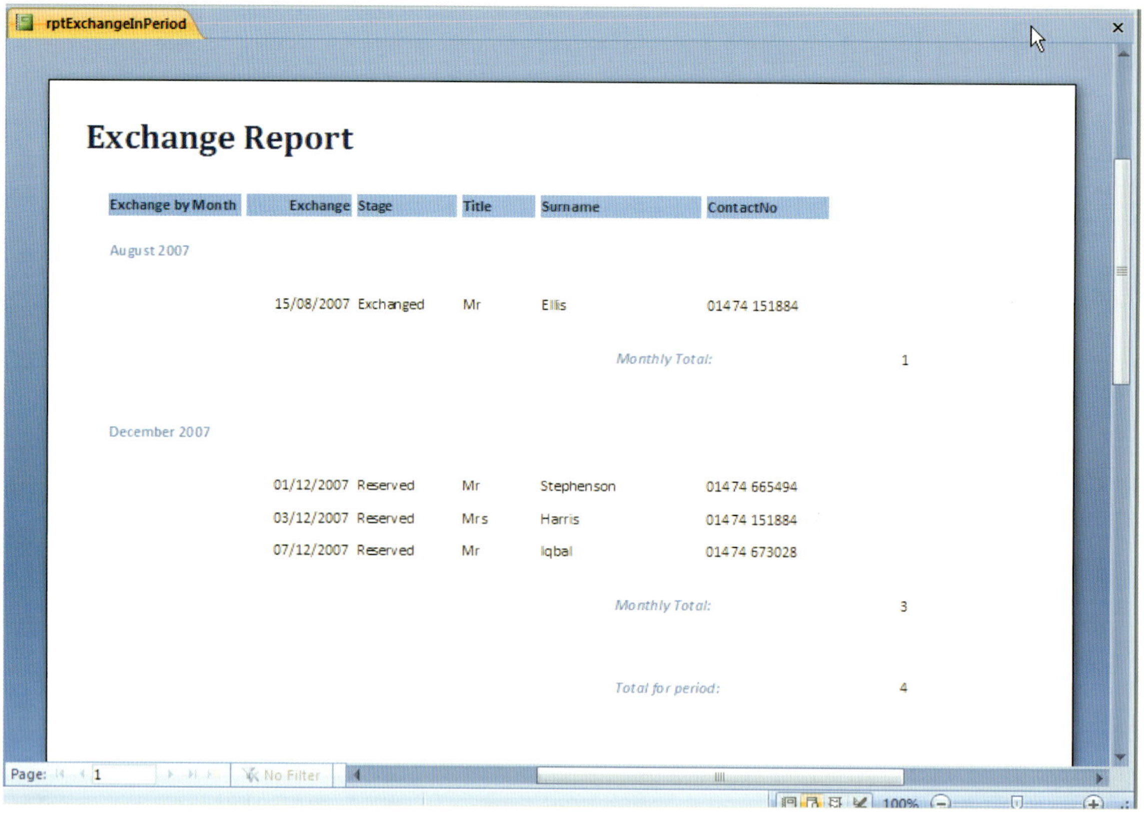

Figure 14.16

Inserting the date in the title

It would be useful if the date range of the report appears in the report title. We'll do this now:

- Go to **Design View** by clicking the **View** button and selecting **Design View**.
- Click the button for the **Text Box control** (see Figure 14.9) on the **Report Design Tools**, **Design** tab and drag out a field in the **Report Header**.
- Change the text in the **Text Box** from **Unbound** to **[Enter start date]**.
- Add a second text box to the right of the first, and enter the text **[Enter end date]**. Access will warn you that no such field exists: it doesn't because you have to supply these dates in a parameter query. All is well!
- Delete one of the labels, and change the other to say ***to***.
- Now change the fonts and rearrange the report to look like Figure 14.17.

Reminder:
Don't forget to enter the square brackets too!

Tip:
When you run the report, the dates you enter should now appear in the Report Header. If they don't, go back and check that the text you have written on the report is exactly the same as the text you wrote in square brackets in qryExchangeIn-Period.

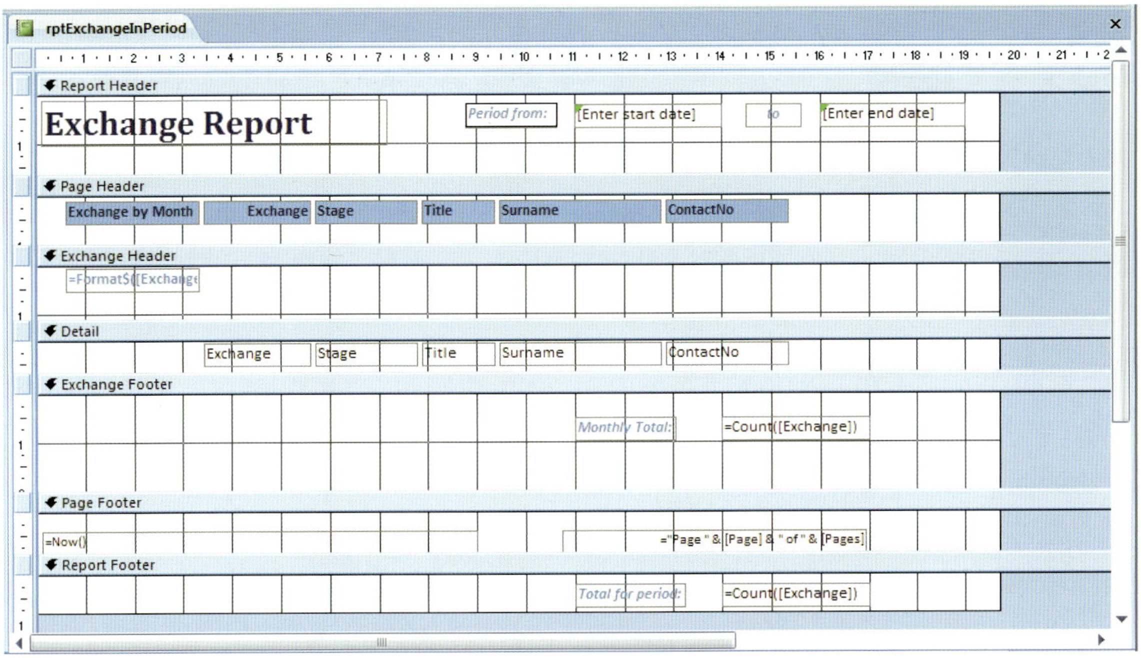

Figure 14.17

Click the **Print Preview** icon to check that these fields work.

Save and close your report.

Exercise

It would be nice to have a report based on **qryHouseStyle** which would print out names of customers interested in a particular house style. This would be useful when new plots are released, and the sales staff need to contact customers who might be interested in those plots.

Try and create this report using the **Report Wizard** just as you did for the report above, saving it as **rptHouseStyle**. When you have created the report, edit the labels and move around the fields so that they look like Figure 14.18.

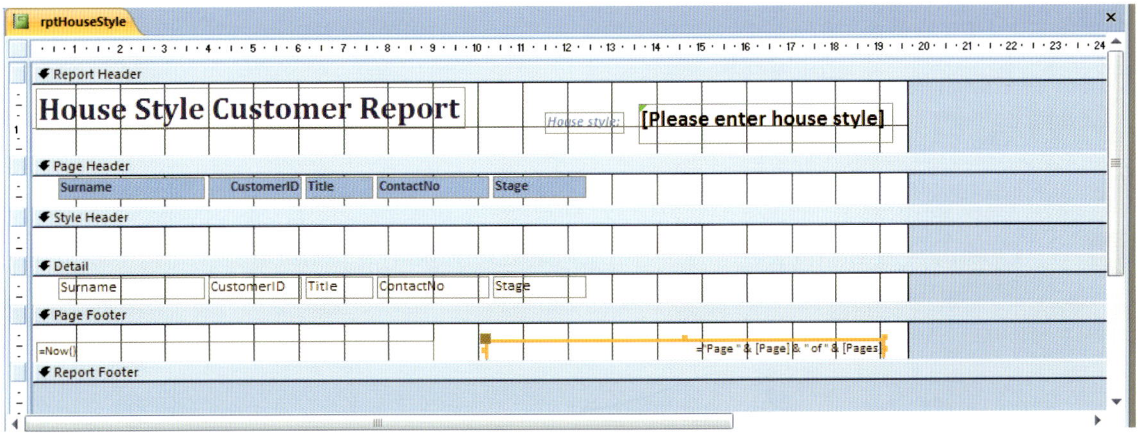

Figure 14.18

Save and close your report – you will need it in the next chapter.

Chapter 15 – Creating a Menu

This is the fun part. You've done the hard work creating forms and reports, and now you need to make the whole database a bit more user-friendly.

By creating a menu, you can hide from the user the inner workings of your database such as the database window.

Before creating the menu in Access, you need to plan out the **menu structure**.

Menu structure

The basic menu structure we will develop is shown in Figure 15.1.

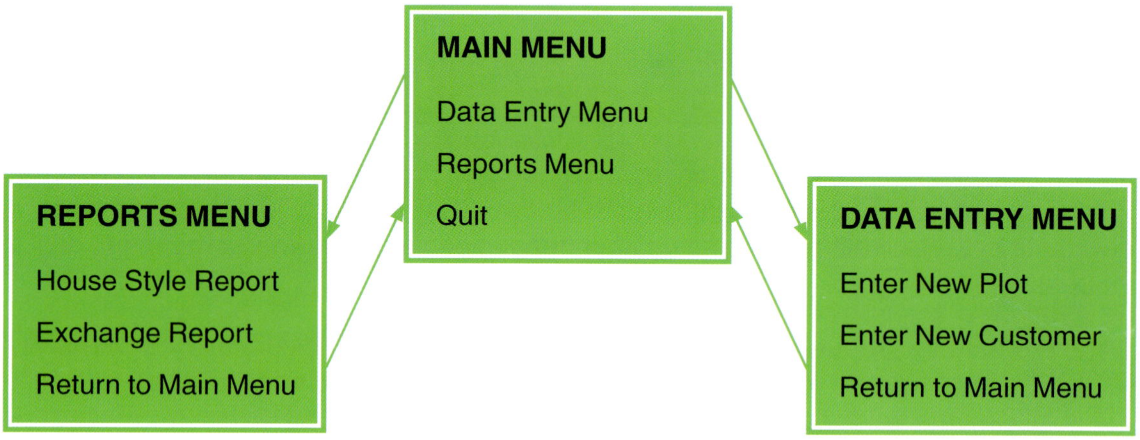

Figure 15.1

Switchboard Manager

The quickest way to create a menu in Access is to use the **Switchboard Manager**.

Open the Switchboard Manager by switching to the **Database Tools** tab, **Switchboard Manager**.

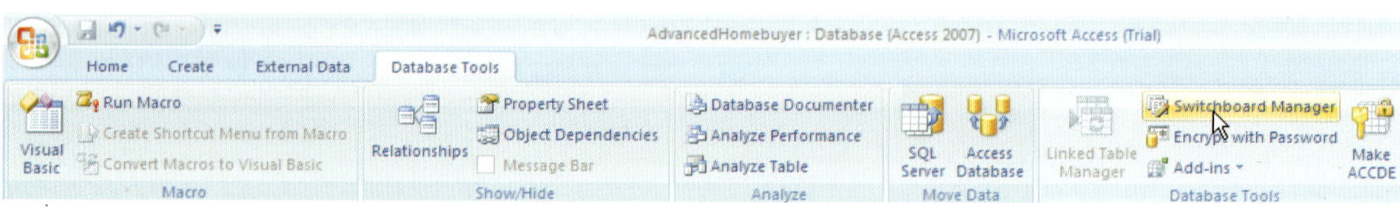

Figure 15.2

Because you haven't created a switchboard yet, you will get the following message:

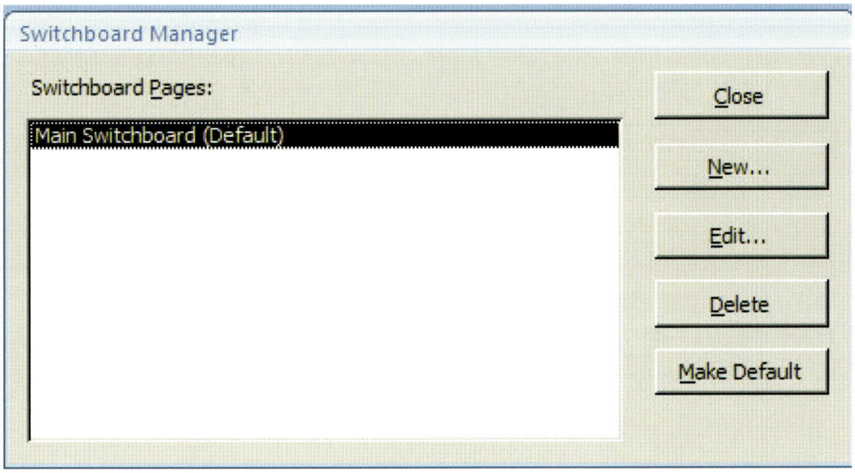

Figure 15.3

- Click **Yes** and the **Switchboard Manager** window opens.

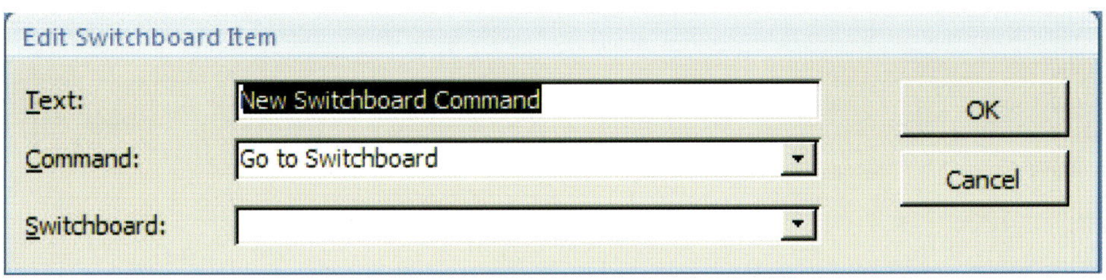

Figure 15.4

It is easiest to start by creating the two submenus before the main menu, so first we will create the **Data Entry Menu**.

- Click **New**, and enter **Data Entry Menu** as the switchboard page name. Click **OK**.
- Now edit this menu: select **Data Entry Menu** and click **Edit**.
- Click **New**, and the **Edit Switchboard Item** window appears.

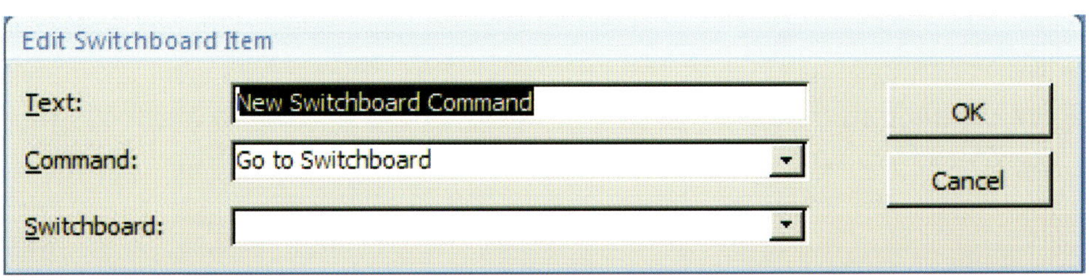

Figure 15.5

In this window you specify the text that appears next to the menu button, and the action that the button will perform. We want it to open the **frmPlot** form.

- Enter **Enter New Plot** as the text.

- Select **Open Form in Add Mode** as the **Command**.
- Select **frmPlot** as the form and click **OK**.

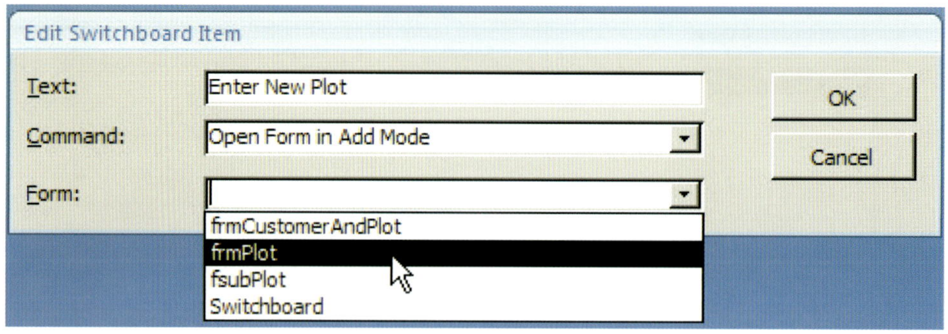

Figure 15.6

- Create another menu item on the **Data Entry Menu** called **Log New Customer**, which opens the **frmCustomerAndPlot** form.

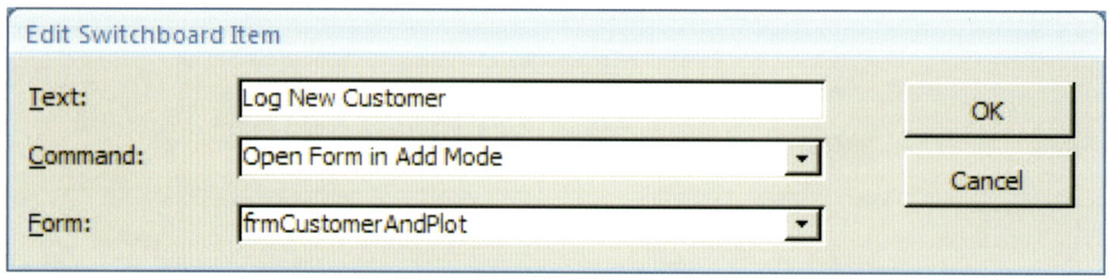

Figure 15.7

- Click **Close** on the **Edit Switchboard Page** dialogue box.

Navigating between menus

On every menu you must have a button to get back to the main menu – or you'll get stuck on one menu. You create this the same way as the **Open Form** buttons you created above, only this time the **Command** will be **Go To Switchboard**.

- First of all, rename the **Main Switchboard** as **Main Menu** by selecting it and clicking **Edit**. Now change the name in the **Switchboard Name** field.
- Click **Close**.
- Create an item on the **Data Entry Menu** called **Return to Main Menu**, with command **Go To Switchboard**. The Switchboard will be **Main Menu**.

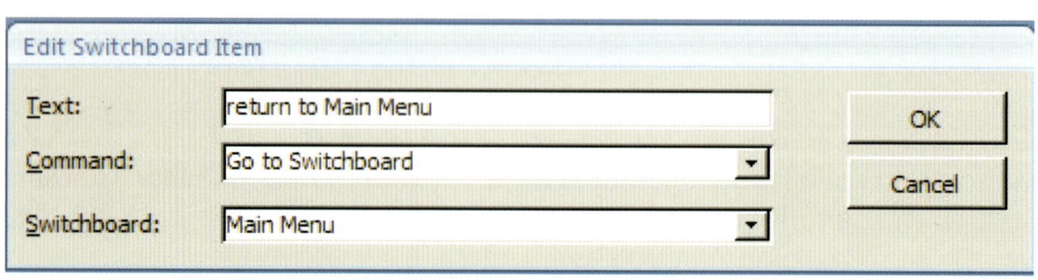

Figure 15.8

Creating the reports/queries menu

Now try and create the **Reports Menu** in the same way you did the **Data Entry Menu**.

The **House Style Report** should open report **rptHouseStyle**.

The **Exchange Report** should open **rptExchangeInPeriod**.

There must also be an item named **Return to Main Menu**.

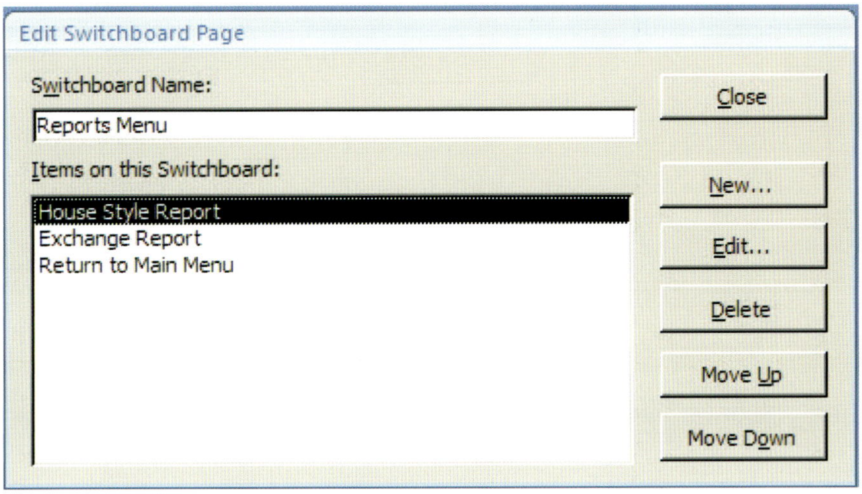

Figure 15.9

Make sure all the menu items have the right names then return to the **Switchboard Manager** window.

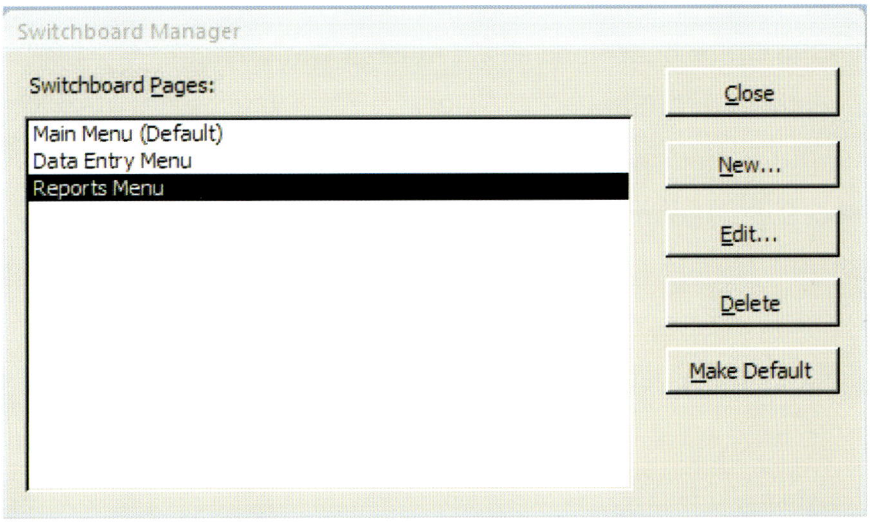

Figure 15.10

Creating the main menu

You do this in exactly the same way. All the items on this menu will have commands **Go To Switchboard**, except the **Quit** item which will specify **Exit Application**.

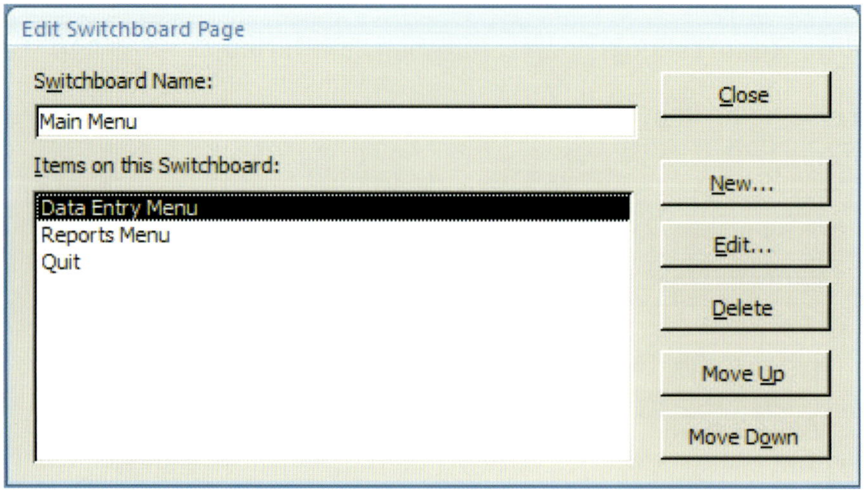

Figure 15.11

- When you have created the menu, close the **Switchboard Manager** by clicking **Close**.

Startup options

Now you have a menu, it would make sense to make it appear automatically when you load the **AdvancedHomebuyer** database. You can do this by editing the **Startup** options.

- Click the **Office** button and select **Access Options**.
- Select **Current Database**.
- Enter **AdvancedHomebuyer database** as the **Application Title**.
- Select **Switchboard** from the drop-down list under **Display Form**.

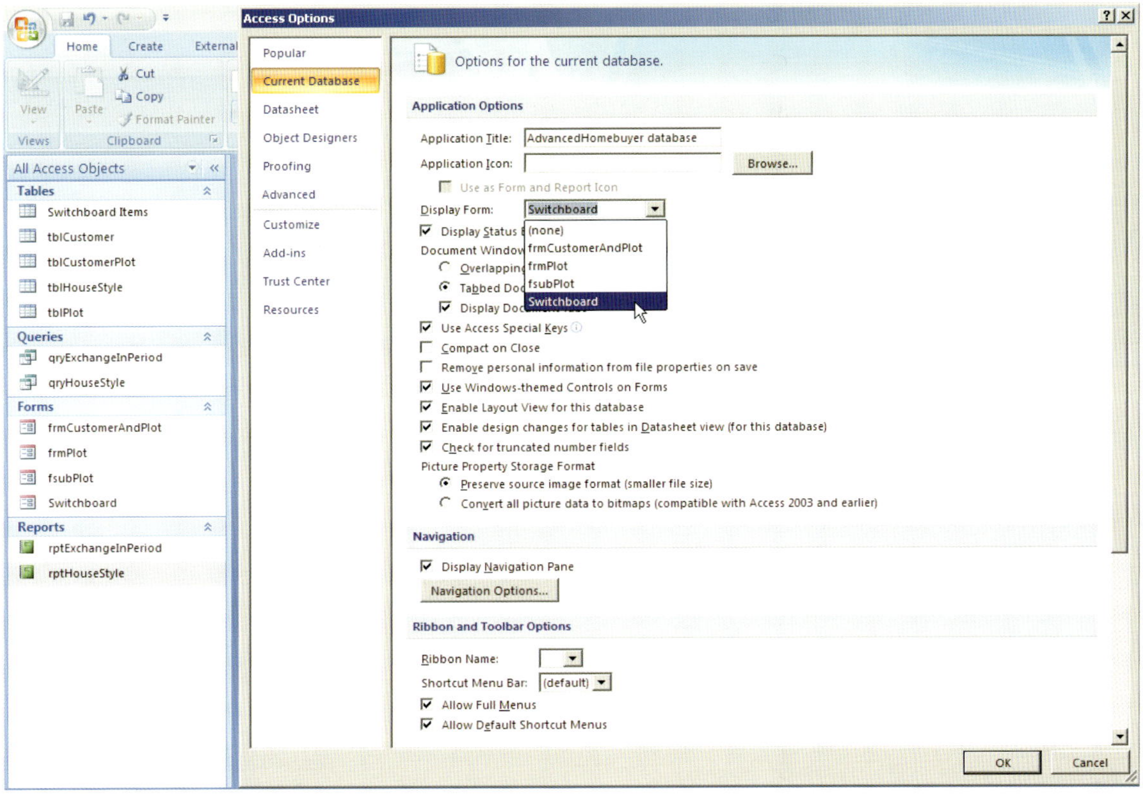

Figure 15.12

Click **OK**.

Testing

You should test your completed menu. Close your database and open it again to check that the menu automatically appears.

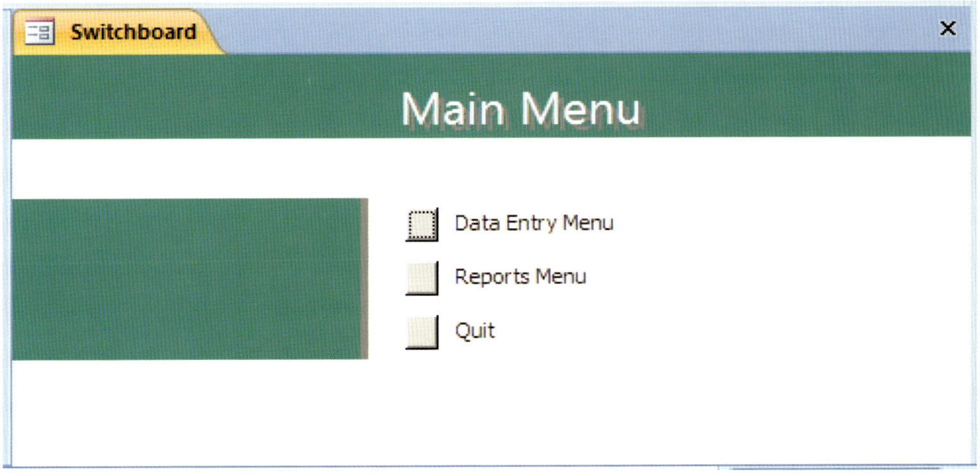

Figure 15.13

When you are happy that everything works correctly, you can save and close your database.

All done!

Index

attributes
- primary key 61
- relationships 58–9, 62–3

AutoNumber 6
- primary key 14, 24, 28, 31

blank database 10–12

combo boxes 92–5

command buttons 84–6

composite (compound) key 60, 62, 68–9

data
- deleting 26–7, 29, 34
- editing 26–7, 28
- entering 23–6, 92–8
- finding 26–7, 28
- menus 114–19
- queries 40–6
- reports 47–55
- types 6–7, 28
- validation 30–4
- warning 73

Datasheet View 13, 21–9

dates, reports 112–13

default values 69

deleting
- data 26–7, 29, 34
- fields 19
- records 26–7, 29, 34

Design View 13–14, 23

drop-down lists 92–5

editing
- data 26–7, 28
- relationships 73
- subforms 91–8
- tables 17–20

entering
- data 23–6, 92–8
- fields 15–16

entities, relationships 58–61, 62–3

Esc (keyboard)
- deleting records 34
- validation 33, 34

fields 4, 6
- adding 51–5
- deleting 19
- entering 15–16
- inserting 18–19
- moving 19
- naming 8
- Number 66
- selecting 7, 41–2
- width 24

finding data/records 26–7, 28

flat file databases 56–7

footers, reports 108–13

formatting
- columns 38–9
- datasheets 36–9

forms 75–86
- creating 75–9
- Form View 78–9
- modifying 79–84
- subforms 87–98

headers, reports 108–13

hiding/unhiding columns 37–8

inserting fields 18–19

key field *see* primary key

linking tables 59–61, 63, 89–90

list boxes 79–84, 93

loading Access 9–12

menus 114–19

naming conventions 8, 43, 48, 62–3

Navigation pane 16, 17
- Shutter Bar 23–4

Number field 66

planning 5–8

presenting data *see* reports

primary key 15, 20
- attributes 61
- AutoNumber 14, 24, 28, 31
- composite (compound) key 60, 62, 68–9
- relationships 59–61

Print Preview
- datasheets 36–7
- reports 51

printing
- datasheets 36–9
- reports 55

queries 40–6
- advanced 99–103
- criteria 42–4, 101–3
- menus 114–19
- reports 104–5
- saving 43, 46
- selecting fields 41–2
- sorting results 45

record selectors 27, 29, 84

records 4
- adding 29
- deleting 26–7, 29, 34
- finding 26–7, 28
- sorting 35–6

referential integrity, relationships 72

relational database design 56–61

relationships 58–61
- attributes 58–9, 62–3
- creating 71–2
- editing 73
- entities 58–61, 62–3
- primary key 59–61
- referential integrity 72
- saving 74
- setting up 70–4
- subforms 87
- types 58
- window 70–1

reports 47–55, 104–13
- adding fields 51–5
- creating 105–8
- dates 112–13
- footers 108–13
- headers 108–13
- menus 114–19
- Print Preview 51
- printing 55
- queries 104–5
- titles 49–51

Ribbon 12

row selectors 16, 19, 68

rules, validation 30–4

Run Time View 13

saving
- queries 43, 46
- relationships 74
- tables 16–17

searching *see* finding

security options 22–3
- validation 31

Shutter Bar, Navigation pane 23–4

sorting
- query results 45
- records 35–6

Startup, menus 118–19

structure
- database 7, 12, 62–3
- Design View 23
- menus 114
- tables 13–17

subforms 87–98
- creating 88–90
- editing 91–8
- relationships 87

Switchboard Manager 114–19

tab order 95

tables 4
- creating 13–16, 62–9
- editing 17–20
- formatting 36–9
- linking 59–61, 63, 89–90
- printing 36–9
- saving 16–17
- sorting 35–6
- structure 13–17
- views 13–14

templates 9

Undo 19

user interface 75
- menus 114–19

validation
- data 30–4
- Esc (keyboard) 33, 34
- rules 30–4
- security options 31

views
- switching 55
- tables 13–14

warning, data 73

width, fields 24

window
- database 12
- relationships 70–1